The
Enviro
Guide t
Garden
Pest Control

Ken March

LONDON

IAN ALLAN LTD

Editor: Sandra Forty

The photographs on front cover,
pages 2, 46 (bottom), and 94 are
reproduced courtesy Bloom's of
Bressingham.

First published 1991

ISBN 0 7110 1924 X

Published by Ian Allan Ltd,
Shepperton, Surrey; and printed
by Ian Allan Printing Ltd at their
works at Coombelands in
Runnymede, England

Contents

 # **Preface**

It is perhaps idealistic to believe that simply leaving garden plants to fend for themselves, with the natural forces of Mother Nature to take account of the control of pests and diseases, provides an acceptable answer to all gardeners' problems. Nevertheless, as soon as man intervenes in the cultivation of plants by using monoculture techniques or systems more convenient to his needs, the natural balance is disturbed and pest and disease control can be a real problem.

Various techniques are discussed in this book from the use of relatively 'environment friendly' materials to the use of natural deterrents and controls to help you enjoy the pleasures of gardening, whilst suggesting ways to deal with problems posed by pest and disease organisms.

Many of these ideas I use myself in my own garden, which despite the moderate proportions of the plot, is a mixture of ornamental, wildlife garden and play area for my three young sons.

Care for the environment has always been a particular passion of mine, which grew from the early days in my career when I was Technical Manager for Europe's leading producer of house plants, where I was very much involved in field trials for the comprehensive range of pesticides being produced. My own interest in wildlife conservation and other environmental issues has influenced my concern for the wider use of pest and disease control measures that are more in harmony with our fragile world.

Apart from working extensively with houseplants, my career has involved working with Fisons Horticulture, where I spent several years covering more comprehensively various aspects of the horticulture industry from turf care to salad crops, cut flowers, fruit, arboriculture and hardy nursery stock production. My growing interest in garden plants led me to a move to Blooms of Bressingham , one of Britain's leading producers of hardy nursery stock — alpines, herbaceous perennials, conifers and shrubs.

As public concern for environmental issues grows at a similar time to the increasing enthusiasm for gardening, it is perhaps timely that apart from gardening with a wildlife theme, more natural methods for dealing with pest and disease problems, including organic chemicals, are worthy of consideration.

There really is no absolutely right way for each problem, rather an informed choice should be made that is appropriate to the situation and crop. Nevertheless, the responsibilities of each of us are real and any intervention with the environment, even within the boundaries of our own gardens, can have disastrous consequences if little thought or concern is exercised when control procedures are carried out using materials that are less 'environment friendly' and are possibly more persistent.

Each and every one of us has a real responsibility for our surroundings in almost everything we do, from the resources that we use, to how we use them. In enjoying the satisfying and rewarding interest of gardening, we should be acutely aware of green issues. I very much hope that the information and tips contained in this book will prove to be of positive use.

Finally, I am indebted to friends and acquaintances in the Ministry of Agriculture, Fisheries and Food, Henry Doubleday Research Association, Royal Society of the Protection of Birds, Worldwide Fund for Nature, Suffolk Wildlife Trust, Greenpeace and Friends of the Earth for either their help or inspiration. I am however more indebted to my family for their tolerance and patience, whilst I have been involved with the researching, writing and typing of this manuscript.

Ken March

Introduction

Whether one cultivates plants for food or pleasure it is a well known fact that you never stop learning about them. Part of this learning process involves not only ensuring that plants are adequately watered and nourished, but that any hindrance to their growth and maturity is rapidly dealt with before any damage occurs or yield is reduced.

It is for this reason that the control of pests and diseases of ornamental and food crops is vitally important. It would seem that tackling the problem of controlling pests infecting one's treasured plants should be a relatively easy problem to resolve. Unfortunately however a visit to the local garden centre, garden shop or chemist can end in confusion with the vast array of products claiming to cure anything from the common greenfly to the dreaded red spider mite.

However, the true environmentally aware organic gardener is committed to cultivating plants naturally and relies entirely upon natural predators and parasites, as well as the use of guard plants to control pests and diseases. The true natural gardener will never spray chemicals, even organic products and through natural cultural expertise helps to prevent pests and diseases by growing sturdy healthy plants that are naturally more resistant to problems.

The organic gardener will combine the use of natural factors with organic pesticides and fertiliser products to cultivate plants, whilst still being absolutely committed to a responsible environmental attitude.

Unfortunately there are other gardeners who will use any product to aid their labours, whatever the origin of the material. However, many people from this category are becoming more aware of green issues and are perhaps beginning to show interest in becoming more selective about what products to use.

Reflecting the interest in a more 'healthy' style of living, with particular attention being given to wholefood, many people are becoming more environmentally aware and prefer to use products that are perceived as being safer for the environment. For this reason the 'return to nature' has inspired an increased interest in pesticides of a natural or organic origin.

This philosophy represents a dramatic shift from postwar days when new pesticides such as DDT appeared on the scene. DDT and chemicals such as aldrin and dieldrin come from a family of chemicals known as organo-chlorines which were initially hailed as one of mankind's greatest achievements. Following their introduction the use of synthetic pesticides dramatically increased and were made available to the consumer in all sorts of clever formulations and materials. The enthusiasm that existed to control the scourge of insect pests manifested itself in a myriad of ingenious ways and various dusts, powders and potions were dispensed liberally all around the home. Apart from hand-pumped spray cans that looked like a development of a bicycle pump with a tin can on the end, there were even cardboard cut-out pictures printed to look like a posy or arrangement of flowers in a basket. This was printed both sides, impregnated with DDT and adorned many a dining room or kitchen as it was suspended from the ceiling light.

Unfortunately, unbeknown to people at the time, this chemical family had a strength or benefit that was also to be its downfall in terms of popularity and use. Organo-chlorines are very stable and persistent chemicals and do not break down rapidly to safer chemicals; this persistence was initially seen as a benefit in terms of controlling insect pests, by virtue of the fact that it stayed around for a long time increasing the risk of pests coming into contact with it being poisoned, but it had a very nasty side effect.

The level of persistence of organo-chlorine pesticides was found to have a disastrous effect upon wildlife and the general ecology. Probably for the first time the effect of food-chain poisoning was graphically illustrated to the detriment of wildlife and the general horror of ecologists and conservationists. Whether on land or in water, the results were frightening.

Although small amounts of the chemicals were thought to have a low level of toxicity, it was proved that the residues would accumulate within the body tissues of animals and for that matter man. Just like the song about the old lady who swallowed a fly, so the food chain problem manifested itself.

Insects that had been exposed to organo-chlorine insecticides were consumed by small mammals or birds. These in turn were preyed upon by larger mammals or birds, all of the time with the residues accumulating inside the bodies of the predators. Even fish were poisoned as they consumed poisoned food or were exposed to residues that had been washed into rivers from over-spray, drift or drainage from treated crops.

These severely detrimental effects of organo-chlorines on the environment resulted in a rapid loss of popularity and increased concern from the increasingly informed consumer about the use of pesticides of such a persistent nature.

Following World War 2 the technology that was developed to produce nerve poisons, that were thankfully not used during the war, was employed to refine synthetic chemicals that would enable man to attack insect pests that preyed upon his crops and thereby to increase yield and quality. So were born the

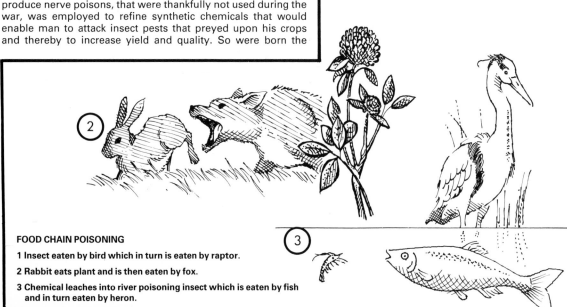

FOOD CHAIN POISONING

1 Insect eaten by bird which in turn is eaten by raptor.

2 Rabbit eats plant and is then eaten by fox.

3 Chemical leaches into river poisoning insect which is eaten by fish and in turn eaten by heron.

All drawings by Richard Armstrong

family of chemicals known as organo-phosphorous chemicals. Pesticides such as parathion, malathion and dimethoate are typical examples of these.

Unlike the organo-chlorine family of insecticides, organo-phosphorous chemicals were initially welcomed as being 'safer' for the environment. However, dependent upon the chemical, the relative degree of poisoning ability or toxicology could often be very high.

Organo-phosphorous pesticides work directly on the insects' nervous system and are very rapid in effect. However, it is a sobering thought to remember that, just like insects, we too have a nervous system and are therefore equally susceptible to the effects of nerve poisons. Care therefore with application and handling is always an important point to be aware of, especially with such chemicals — even with those that are known to be much less toxic than others.

A major benefit of organo-phosphorous chemicals lies in the fact that they are not as stable as organo-chlorines and are therefore much less likely to persist in the environment. After a relatively short period, sometimes only hours, the chemical begins to deteriorate and break down to safer by-products, thereby reducing the possible long-term risk problems.

The proliferation of man-made pesticides has not always been for the reasons of environmental issues, but also from commercial necessity. A phenomenon was observed many years back, when repeated doses of pesticide applications failed to adequately control insect pests. Scientists soon discovered that the clever little bugs had simply become resistant to the man-made poisons. In fact it could be said that these same chemicals had acted almost as an evolutionary stimulus. Applications of sub-lethal doses, or in other words insufficient chemical to kill a pest, had the effect of separating the strong

Left:
When spraying without a surfactant (wetting agent), even coverage is very difficult. Note the surface tension effect on the leaves, illustrated by the globules of spray solution.
K. March

Right:
The addition of a wetting agent enables the foliage to be effectively covered and thoroughly wetted. Note the absence of 'globules' and more even spray coverage. *K. March*

from the weak. This forced effect of the survival of the fittest meant that surviving insect pests would give birth to offspring that would inherit the resistance.

Within a relatively short space of time (sometimes only a few weeks in the case of an insect with a short life cycle such as a greenfly) the population of resistant pests could reach plague proportions that could not be controlled using the chemical that effected the change.

Even chemicals from the same family often had no effect and so the scientists' search for increasingly sophisticated chemicals continues to this day. More recently chemicals such as sevin and pirimicarb have appeared, originating from a newer family of pesticides called carbamates. So sophisticated have some of these chemicals become, that their very mode of action and sometimes selectivity has to be acknowledged as being ingenious

In applying a chemical pesticide to an infested plant, one supposes that the pest is poisoned by the chemical droplets from the spray mist adhering to the insect and killing it. Whilst this is true to some extent, many spray chemicals rely on the material settling on the leaf tissue which in turn will be consumed by the pest, thereby poisoning itself.

However, both rely on good spray coverage, or in other words an adequate level of the spray chemical 'sticking' to a major part of the surface area of the plant's foliage, including upper and lower leaf surfaces, as well as contacting the actual pest itself. This can be very difficult to achieve and whilst efficient sprayers may improve the coverage, they will not on their own solve the problem of sticking the chemical to the leaf. For this reason chemicals called wetting agents or surfactants have been developed. These work like a detergent in helping to break down the natural surface tension of the spray solution carried by water to improve the level of coverage. This has been particularly important when pesticides have been applied to leaves with a

hairy, powdery or waxy surface, which can be extremely difficult to wet effectively.

Apart from the practical problem of applying a pesticide to a large part of the plant's surface area in an attempt to effect control of a pest, just think of the difficulties when attempting to treat a large shrub, tree or simply a plant with dense foliage. Similarly a pest such as an aphid can be difficult to locate when the young leaves curl and twist in reaction to the attack and in so doing provide a safer haven for the pest.

To deal with this problem, chemicals have been developed which are systemic or trans-laminar in action. Systemic insecticides are actually absorbed by the plant and are transported systemically, or in other words throughout the plant's system, producing poisonous sap and plant tissue that is toxic to the insect pest. As soon as the pest consumes the sap, or plant tissue, it absorbs the poison and is poisoned and killed.

Alternatively a chemical that works in a trans-laminar fashion simply passes through the leaf and poisons insects on the other side of the leaf surface that the spray poison was deposited on.

In either case systemic or trans-laminar chemicals need not be applied so thoroughly as chemicals that are effective only in a contact mode. Sadly, this is a disadvantage in terms of effectiveness in comparing organic pesticides against man-made insecticides. Unfortunately, organic pesticides are usually only effective as contact insecticides, whereas man-made chemicals can be much more sophisticated in terms of their systemic activity.

Another disadvantage of organic pesticides is that they are rarely selective. Treating aphids, or greenfly, for example can be a problem if you use an organic insecticide during daylight hours, when bees are around, as they too can be poisoned. Obviously, one would therefore need to spray an organic pesticide in the evening after the bees have returned to their hives, to avoid poisoning them as well as other useful insects.

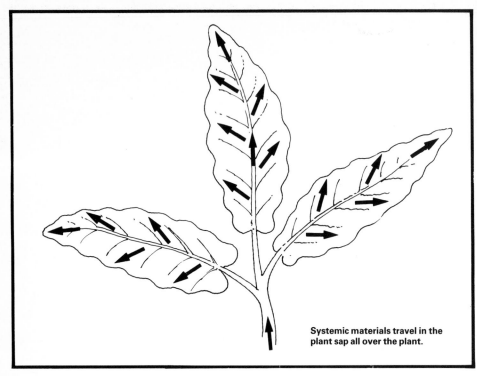

Systemic materials travel in the plant sap all over the plant.

However, certain man-made pesticides are so sophisticated that they discriminate between the pest and beneficial insects. Pirimicarb has been promoted as a chemical that controls aphids, whilst not harming the natural predators of aphids such as ladybirds larvae, as well as a large number of beneficial mites and insects.

Nevertheless for the discriminating environmentalist concerned with only the use of organic materials, a compromise has to be accepted in terms of the likely lower level of effectiveness of control gained in favour of using materials that are from a natural origin, with perceived environmental benefits.

Controlling pests for the damage that they do in a direct sense also needs closer understanding, for some pests can cause considerably more damage in an indirect way. Aphids for example can severely distort and damage young growth including new shoots, leaves and flower buds. They can also act

Right:
Pirimicarb is a selective man-made insecticide that is effective in controlling aphids and yet is harmless to predatory ladybirds and other insects such as bees.

as a vector or carrier of plant viruses which can be particularly troublesome on such crops as strawberries, blackcurrants, redcurrants, gooseberries and potatoes.

Plant viruses cannot be cured and infected plants must be dug up and burnt to reduce the likelihood of the further spread of infection. For this reason alone it is imperative that plants prone to infestations with pests, such as aphids are sprayed regularly to prevent the build-up of aphid populations, rather than just spraying when the pest is seen and the damage has possibly already been done.

Plant viruses manifest themselves in a number of ways, not all of which are, oddly enough, alarming. Indeed, some variegations and leaf pattern effects on ornamental plants are believed to be caused by viruses that 'damage' the plant in a pleasing way to the gardener such as attractively striped tulips. Vigour may be reduced in plants that are affected in this way, although this may not always be the case. The growth rate and habit of 'infected' varieties may be similar to a comparable 'uninfected' variety.

However, leaving ornamental plants to one side, the result of viruses on food crops can be severe. Apart from deforming the foliage, in the form of crinkling or curling leaves, the effect of a virus can cause a mosaic patterning of the foliage. These symptoms are not however the main problem, for in food crops the effect of a viral infection is to markedly reduce the yield, often with dire commercial consequences for the professional grower. Even the amateur can suffer a severe loss of cropping potential and for this reason plant viruses should not be taken too lightly and drastic action must be taken to destroy infected plants to reduce the likelihood of spread.

The organic gardener is therefore faced with a complex problem in dealing with the profitable and satisfying production and cultivation of plants for culinary and ornamental use, whilst attempting to abide by a code of practice that does not compromise the beliefs and benefits of plant husbandry the organic way.

It is not enough just to simply attempt to control pests with a limited range of organic chemicals, when the pests are only discovered at what is quite often an advanced stage of infestation. Due to the shortcomings in terms of activity and lack of systemic activity of organic materials, regular inspections of the plants must be carried out and even precautionary preventative treatments considered at times of the year when there is an increased level of probability that insect pest attacks could occur.

Simply spraying when an infestation is seen is also unlikely to be sufficient. Not only do insects develop through various forms of life-cycle, at some stages of which the pest is unaffected by the treatment, but you would be very lucky indeed to kill off all of the pests on the plant with one spray treatment. This is due to problems of spray coverage and contact as mentioned previously. It is therefore important to mount a spraying programme that consists of several applications, to not only account for any pests that might have missed the first treatment but also young emerging adults developing from the various life-cycles.

A further method of controlling insect pests is biological control, which employs the use of parasitic or predatory insects or mites to control the problem. These can be very effective if used correctly and managed properly, although it has to be realised that for biological control to be effective you have to accept that a certain level of pest population needs to be tolerated for the parasite or predator to live on. In simple terms, if the pest is completely eradicated then the predator or parasite will starve and decline and may not recover in sufficient numbers to control the pest when a re-infestation occurs.

Biological control is particularly effective when used within a controlled environment which can be well managed and maintained, such as within a glasshouse. Under this type of regime whitefly can be well controlled by the use of parasitic *Encarsia formosa* wasps and red spider mites can be controlled by the predatory mite *Phytoseiulus persimilis*.

In the case of the parasitic wasp Encarsia, the wasp lays its eggs in the larval scales of the whitefly which then turn black instead of the usual white appearance. Having successfully parasitised the larval stage of the whitefly, the parasitic wasp emerges and within a relatively short time lays eggs in other whitefly scales, thereby keeping the population in check.

The predatory mite simply chases and consumes red spider mites and again maintains a level of balance.

By this method a number of insect pests can be controlled, but again it must be stressed that for biological control to be effective a level of population of the pest has to be tolerated, as well as a certain degree of damage and possibly reduced yield.

Damage caused to plants by insect pests can vary greatly from minor blotchiness and discoloration to massive deformation and necrosis (die-back). Pests such as whitefly can sustain a high population infestation, whilst at the same time causing fairly minimal damage. The only sign of their activity is minor discoloration and blotchiness of the foliage.

Aphids on the other hand can be a real nuisance, as their stabbing mouthparts are efficiently employed on the soft young tissue of new shoots, leaves and flower buds. As these emerge, the damage becomes magnified as the parts expand and grow and the leaves twist, curl and develop in a quite grotesque fashion.

Caterpillars and some other pests with large biting mouth-parts can make short work of a plant and leave great holes or stripped foliage. However, in many respects the damage caused by tiny mites such as red spider mites, or two-spotted mites can be equally traumatic to a plant, albeit not so visible in the early stages of attack. Spider mites are almost microscopic in size and feed mainly on the undersides of leaves resulting in severe yellowish discoloration and mottling. This is followed by the foliage taking on a hard and cupped appearance as the leaf begins to curl. At this stage the foliage may well become necrotic with large areas of the leaf and leaf edges dying and turning brown, followed later by leaf drop.

Apart from the various effects shown by plants suffering from a pest attack, there is frequently another associated problem. Quite often a plant may be covered by honeydew, a sticky sugary substance excreted as a waste product by such pests as aphids and scale insects. This itself is unsightly, but the situation can become far worse when the honeydew is then covered by sooty mould — a black fungal growth that lives on the honeydew. This looks like patches of black powder sprinkled on the sticky patches and is really quite horrid and completely spoils the appearance of a plant, or its flowers or fruit.

Tomatoes in particular not only look quite unappetising when covered with sooty mould, but feel revolting as the fruit is sticky and dirty when harvested.

Sooty mould can relatively easily be washed off fruit spoiled in this way by simply washing with a mild warm solution of soap or detergent, prior to being rinsed with clean water. Affected plants, especially ornamental plants, may need to be gently sponged or wiped with cottonwool or a soft cloth moistened with a warm solution of soap or detergent. Similarly, after cleaning, the leaves should be rinsed with clean water.

Pests can therefore be a real problem requiring consideration in terms of treatment to control them to avoid reduced yield, inferior vigour and performance, or simply sickly appearance. Used with care and consideration organic chemicals and possibly biological control methods can be employed to reduce the problem and improve the plant's health and welfare.

However, remember that plants are part of nature and should be considered in harmony with it. Cultivating plants can sometimes be seen as disturbing this harmony and the importance of trying to maintain a balance should not be underestimated. It is imperative to try to ensure that the garden environment is well balanced with areas allowed to encourage and promote wildlife to allow nature to assist in the control of pest problems naturally.

There are indeed many natural controls of pest and disease problems, but through our interference the balance is disturbed and pest control becomes more difficult for nature to deal with. Ideally, everything should be in balance, but, as it rarely is, we often have to resort to the use of poisons, albeit organic ones, to remove problems that are to some degree of our own making.

1
Types of Sprayer

Probably the most common form of chemical application is the use of the technique termed spraying. Applying chemicals in spray form may be carried out in various ways from ultra low volume (ULV) to high volume, depending upon the chemical, crop and situation.

Although high volume is certainly the most popular and regularly used, with the advent of improved technological development of sprayers and chemical formulations, ultra low sprayers are now beginning to be more widely available. This is especially the case in the commercial horticultural sector. However, due to the use of solvents often acting as carriers for the chemical, this may not be an acceptable method to the organic gardener.

It is therefore most likely that high volume spraying will continue to remain the most popular method of chemical application, but before considering the types of sprayer that can be used, it is worth considering the merits and deficiencies of the various spraying systems.

Ultra low volume

Unlike high volume sprayers that use water as a carrier for the pesticide, ultra low volume sprayers usually make use of a chemical carrier. The effect of this is that rather than many litres of water being used to wet spray plants, a few cubic centimetres of solvent and pesticide are used.

As the chemical is applied to the crop, the solvent evaporates leaving minute droplets of pesticide evenly covering the plant. As the droplets are so tiny and the method of application makes use of air currents, the degree of coverage is normally quite impressive.

The type of sprayer used is also quite different and is certainly most unconventional, usually making use of such things as fans and spinning discs to produce the tiny droplets. Similarly, the chemicals used are also distinctly different and are perhaps more dangerous to handle due to the higher level of concentration of the spray solution and relative level of potency. No mixing or measuring is usually required, which itself is a

Below:
A Turbair Sprite battery-powered ULV sprayer which applies an ultra-fine mist of spray particles carried by air currents around the foliage of plants. *Turbair Ltd*

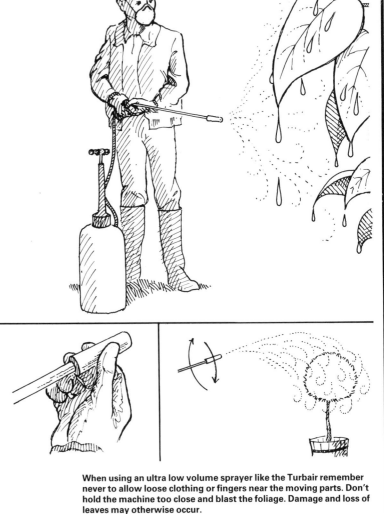

When using an ultra low volume sprayer like the Turbair remember never to allow loose clothing or fingers near the moving parts. Don't hold the machine too close and blast the foliage. Damage and loss of leaves may otherwise occur.

carrier chemical, which is then completely vaporised once the chemical makes contact with the plant. The movement and turbulence of air currents and foliage helps to ensure that a very large part of the leaf surface of the crop is covered.

In obtaining such a good level of coverage the system helps to make the use of organic chemicals much more effective. Some of the first chemicals to be widely and very effectively used through the system were based on pyrethrum and synthetic pyrethrins.

Disease control can also be enhanced due to the improved level of penetration and coverage when using fungicides through the system. This can be a great benefit especially when repetitive spray applications are required to react to the various stages of the disease, or for that matter pest life cycle.

A further benefit of the system is that it is usually faster than conventional high volume spraying and apart from not having to mix the chemicals, the technique is very easy and almost fun to use. The air turbulence from the fan is directed over and to some degree through the crop, taking care not to blast foliage that is too close to the outlet. The effect aimed for should be simply to waft air around the foliage, rather than to subject it to a hurricane force vortex that can at the very least damage leaves and may even cause some defoliation.

Extra care is necessary when using such a system, as apart from injury that could be caused by moving parts, or from hot exhaust systems or gases in the case of petrol-driven systems, it has to be noted that the chemicals are being applied in a much more concentrated form than by high volume spraying. As such it is imperative that the manufacturer's recommendations are closely followed regarding the handling and use of adequate protective clothing, especially including protection from inhaling the chemical mist or vapour.

Apart from the problem of extra care being necessary, there is however a considerable benefit regarding disposal of surplus chemical. Conventional high volume sprayers either run out and need to be refilled with a new mix, or leave you with surplus solution at the end of the spraying operation. Chemicals that are diluted should not be stored more than a few hours as they may start to degrade and lose their potency. This therefore means that other plants that do not need spraying may be sprayed just to use the chemical up. Alternatively, the chemical solution may end up being disposed of in some fashion, normally by being poured onto waste ground. Obviously, the organic gardener would find either a questionable practice and may therefore prefer the alternative offered by the ultra low volume system. When spraying is completed using ultra low volume, the machine is simply switched off and the chemical bottle removed, resealed and safely stored until it is required again.

Left:
A petrol-engined Turbair sprayer being used to treat a field of soft fruit. The more powerful model is ideal for larger areas and field application. *Turbair Ltd*

benefit and the normally ready-to-use formulation is fed directly into the sprayer.

One particular system that is used widely in commercial horticulture makes use of a powered fan and a system of spinning discs onto which the chemical is fed. Due to the high speed of rotating discs and the effect of the vortex-producing fan, the chemical is broken up into a mist of microscopic droplets that waft through the air on the forced air current. This excited volume of air and chemical droplets begins to lose the

As the system is more complex, the maintenance of the sprayer should be restricted to the basics of cleaning, battery charging, fuel and oil filling and little else, unless specified by the manufacturer. No attempt should be made to disassemble the unit and any other maintenance should be carried out by the manufacturer.

The fan on such a system may be powered by a rechargeable battery or directly from mains electricity. It may also be powered by a petrol engine, although this can be rather more noisy, even if it is possibly more powerful.

Finally, the merits and deficiencies of the system must be left to the individual to judge, although perhaps it is worth stressing that the keen organic gardener may have to consider particularly hard. It must be remembered that a solvent is used to carry the chemical and that quite often formulations that are available for the system may make more extensive use of synthetic pyrethrins rather than natural pyrethrum, even though the chemicals are quite similar.

High volume spraying

The most common and popular method of applying pesticides is by the use of high volume sprayers. These make use of water as a carrier and when mixed with the chemical concentrate the resultant solution is sprayed onto the crop.

Coverage of the crop tends to be a limiting factor with this technique, as is adequate wetting of the foliage. Although to some extent both of these problems may be partly alleviated by the use of a surfactant or wetting agent, it always remains a problem in obtaining complete coverage. This is particularly important when using organic pesticides, as the efficacy of the chemical applied to the plant is in direct relationship with its degree of coverage.

A further problem of wet or high volume spraying is that once the solution has been mixed, it should ideally all be used up in the spraying operation. Otherwise, the surplus product should be, as far as possible, safely disposed of. This may mean pouring the solution onto the garden, with obvious detrimental effect to whatever was living in that particular place.

However, high volume spraying is certainly easier, with much less to go wrong, as it is the least technology based – provided of course that the chemical solution is correctly mixed.

The types of sprayer available vary from the small low budget hand-held mister type, to a multitude of powered sprayers for the spectrum of uses. Some directly pressurise the chemical and immediately process it from solution to droplets and direct it onto the crop, whilst others use air to compress the solution and

force it out through the spray nozzle. The former technique requires constant activity to produce the spray, whilst with compressed air the sprayer is pressurised at the start of the spraying operation, leaving the operator free to direct the spray as wished. Ultimately the type of sprayer selected depends upon the preference of the operator and the quantity of plants to be treated.

The small hand-held mister is probably the most effective small sprayer for treating house plants, low-growing garden plants or the odd few specimens. Most misters hold over ½ litre (about a pint) and produce a fine mist, which on some models can be adjusted to a coarser size of droplet. To obtain most effective coverage, the mister should be adjusted to the finest mist setting, as the smaller droplets will most effectively wet the foliage.

Great care must be taken when making up the chemical solution as the margin for error with such a small volume is proportionately larger and damage can easily occur if the solution is made up too strongly. To help ensure adequate mixing, measure half of the water required into the sprayer, before adding the chemical. The mixture should then be thoroughly agitated and mixed before adding the remainder of the water. Take care that the top of the sprayer, comprising the piston-type pump unit, trigger and nozzle assembly is completely secure before finally shaking again.

Before spraying onto the plants, pump the trigger and whilst directing the spray away from you into a place where it can do no harm, adjust the nozzle to produce the best spray pattern of fine mist droplets possible. Once this has been achieved, the spray can then be applied to the crop using a wafting, circular spray pattern to disturb the foliage for maximum penetration and coverage. Spray until run-off, ie when droplets begin to conglomerate on the leaf surface and start to form larger drops that literally run-off to the extremities and tips of leaves.

As the sprayer is usually very cheap and may not have a prolonged life, maintenance tends to be very simple. Following spraying, the sprayer should be thoroughly washed out with clean water, remembering to pump water through the unit as well and taking care to clean the intake filter, if there is one, at the bottom of the intake pipe.

If the nozzle produces a defective spray pattern at any time, unscrew it and rinse it out in a bowl of water. Try not to rinse it under a tap as you could easily wash away the small bits. If the nozzle is blocked, clear the jet with a piece of fine fuse wire. Never blow through a blocked nozzle, as you are dealing with poisons, albeit organic ones.

If the unit fails to pump despite cleaning, the piston pump unit may have worn out and you may need a replacement. However,

Left:
Hand-held misters are ideal for small-scale spraying operations, particularly where just the odd one or two plants need to be treated or a small localised pest or disease problem. *Hozelock*

prior to discarding, try to pump some warm water with a little soft soap in solution through, as this may clear any stubborn blockage or deposit.

The next step up from the small hand-held mister is the pressure sprayer. The great advantage of this type of sprayer is that rather than having to keep pumping the sprayer during the spraying operation, the sprayer is pumped up first and usually lasts for the entire contents of the container.

The pressure sprayer is available in a wide range of sizes to suit a multitude of uses from a small hand-held unit with a capacity of 0.85 litres (about 1.5 pints) to larger units that have a capacity of 7 litres (about 1.5gal) with a carrying strap and spraying lance.

Whatever the capacity of the unit, the sprayer consists of a strong container capable of being pressurised, which is filled according to the manufacturer's instructions to an appropriate

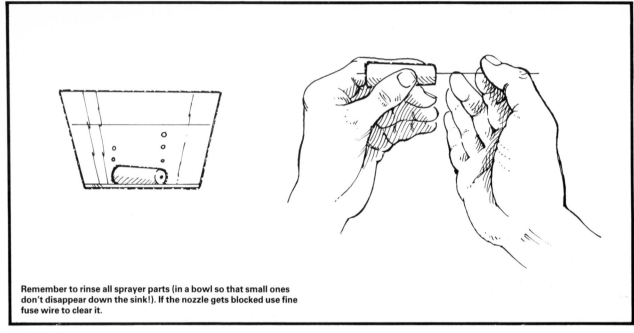

Remember to rinse all sprayer parts (in a bowl so that small ones don't disappear down the sink!). If the nozzle gets blocked use fine fuse wire to clear it.

level. This is important, for failure to observe the recommendations by overfilling could result in a poor spraying performance.

Once filled, the container is then tightly sealed by screwing the top pump unit on to the base and is then compressed by hand pumping. Before starting, check to ensure that the valve, if there is one, is closed on the outlet that feeds the nozzle, otherwise a stream of unwanted spray will be prematurely misdirected.

Having pumped the container an appropriate number of times, again according to instructions, the unit is ready for use. Incidentally, over-pumping may damage the unit and even split the container, whilst under-pumping may result in a feeble spray of coarser droplets providing a poor spray pattern. When the container is pressurised with compressed air, the spray solution is released by either a simple trigger or valve mechanism on the smaller units, or alternatively by a tap or valve mechanism located on a spray lance attached to a flexible pipe on larger units.

Similar to the mister, the pressure sprayer nozzle can normally be adjusted to vary the spray pattern. Models with a brass nozzle offer the added benefit of an even better spray pattern and more precise control over the size of the chemical droplet.

Once the unit is pressurised and the nozzle appropriately adjusted for the desired spray pattern, spraying can begin. Small units with the spray nozzle mounted directly on the sprayer are probably better for small spraying operations, whilst much greater freedom and mobility can be attained with a sprayer with a spraying lance attached. These are particularly good for spraying in the garden amongst plants where the nozzle can be directed where needed. This is ideal for a multitude of spraying tasks and enables the operator to spray in amongst the foliage into all sorts of concealed areas, without having to keep moving the spray container around.

As it is so important to effect good spray coverage when using organic pesticides, it is well worth investing in a better sprayer which has the benefits of a spray lance and preferably brass spray nozzle to give the best possible result. These however, do cost more.

When buying a pressure sprayer, do not buy a cheap unbranded one, as there may be difficulty in obtaining spare parts and the unit may not be as safe as a branded product. A good proprietary model will usually feature a pressure relief valve, which is a useful safety benefit that automatically vents the pressure vessel before it splits.

A problem that gets worse as the size of the sprayer used increases, may be that of wastage as surplus spray material is left at the end of the spraying operation. If you do not have a use for this material, do not leave it in the container as it will only deteriorate and may in some cases damage the sprayer. When this happens it is better to vent the sprayer, as recommended by the manufacturer and dispose of the surplus chemical in a safe manner. However, it is far better to try to ensure that there is no surplus left. Even pouring the chemical over a piece of waste garden away from children, pets, ponds and watercourses, as frequently recommended, still may have localised, detrimental effects upon the immediate environment. If you must do this, dilute the chemical further with water to disperse the poisons more. Never dispose of the chemical by pouring it down the sink or drain or into a ditch, stream or where it could find its way into a watercourse. It is surprising how much harm can be caused by so little chemical – even an organic one.

Similar to the mister, the pressure sprayer should be thoroughly rinsed out after use, pouring away the rinsings onto the garden in the same way that the surplus chemical was disposed of.

Due to the nature of the type of sprayer and the fact that there are more moving parts and more seals and components that could fail or leak in time, it is usually possible to get spare parts to adequately maintain and service the sprayer. This is particularly the case if the sprayer is of a good make such as a Hozelock/ASL sprayer. However, the units are normally very reliable and should give good service for many spraying operations.

If you have a large area to spray then take a look at the non-pressurised knapsack sprayer that can hold a greater capacity of spray solution of up to 9 litres (about 2gal). The pump mechanism is a diaphragm type that provides a near constant spray flow and consistent spray pattern, provided that the hand lever is constantly operated! Whilst one hand is used to pump the unit, the other is used to hold, direct and operate the spray lance.

This type of unit is useful for large spraying operations where the operator needs to move amongst the crop without having to keep picking up the spray container and moving it as the spraying procedure is carried out. However, for those with back problems, beware! Although carrying a pack equivalent to about 9-11kg (20-25lb) is bad enough, consider the problems of keeping balance as the fluid contents move about. Great care therefore needs to be exercised with the larger sprayers of the knapsack type, as they can be difficult for the novice to safely carry and use.

Remember also that on top of any safety recommendations made by the chemical manufacturer, in terms of the handling and use of the pesticides involving whatever safety equipment

Right:
A pressure relief valve is an important safety feature on compressed air sprayers. The valve can be seen on the opposite side of the spray pipe. This prevents the container rupturing in the event of excessive air being pumped in.
Hozelock

Far right:
If weedkillers have to be used, be sure to use a sprayer that is solely used for herbicides. Weedkillers have a nasty habit of leaving residues behind in sprayers that can damage or kill cultivated plants if the sprayer is used for other applications.
Hozelock

is required, it is well worth wearing a waterproof coat or spraying jacket and a waterproof hat such as a sou'wester. Knapsack sprayers of this type are notorious for leaking a little through the vent hole at the top as the operator moves about. It is therefore sensible to take extra care to protect yourself from any contact with the spray chemical, either from any leaks or from spray droplets that could land on the operator, instead of the crop.

Although the true organic gardener will not use herbicides (weedkillers), it is nevertheless worth noting that this type of sprayer is widely used for herbicide application. Instead of a cone-spray nozzle, a fan-spray nozzle is attached which produced a fan-like downward spray of coarser-sized droplets.

It should go without saying that if a sprayer is used for herbicide application, it should never be used afterwards for spraying pesticides onto crops. No matter how thoroughly a sprayer is washed out, it is still possible for the smallest amount of chemical residue from the herbicide to contaminate the pesticide solution, with possible detrimental effects on plants that are sprayed with the solution. Although it will cost more, it is far better to have a sprayer for each type of operation.

If you can afford it, an ideal combination of sprayers would probably consist of a small hand-held mister or pressure sprayer for spraying tasks in the conservatory, greenhouse or for that matter the odd plant or two in the garden and a larger pressure sprayer. Ideally, the larger pressure sprayer should have a carrying strap to make it easier to carry. This larger sprayer should be equipped with a hand-held lance coupled to the sprayer with a flexible pipe, to provide maximum flexibility in the spray operation.

Although dilutor type sprayers are available on the market, which work by being attached to a hosepipe and calibrated for the required dilution rate, they are not as accurate in the control of the integrity of the solution as a pre-mixed spray solution. Dilutor type applicators may be used for pesticides, but are probably better used for the application of fertiliser solutions. There is rarely much of a safety margin when applying pesticides and no risks should be taken. For this reason, conventional sprayers will offer greater efficiency and accuracy when used as directed.

Finally, at the end of the season, take care to ensure that the sprayer is thoroughly washed out, preferably washing through with a dilute soft soap solution, before rinsing and washing out with clean water. The sprayer should then be completely emptied and any traces of water in pipes or nozzles blown through. Failure to do this may result in blockages the following season, to the frustration of the user and the detriment of the sprayer.

2 Methods of Control

To be effective at controlling insect pests with organic pesticides, one has to not only be thorough, but also patient. Obtaining successful control of insect pests using organic pesticides may prove to be rather harder work than resorting to the use of systemic, synthetic insecticides of an inorganic origin. This is mainly due to the need for complete coverage of all parts of the infested plant to obtain effective control.

Pesticides can be applied in a number of ways depending upon the situation, type of infestation and the pest or disease concerned. Applying pesticidal treatments is not just the process of squirting a chemical solution on to a plant in an unplanned fashion. Some thought should be given to the type of formulation to be used and how and when to apply it.

Spraying

Probably the most popular and common method of application is by the use of a spray formulation. Chemical sprays can sometimes be bought ready-mixed in a simple hand sprayer, which can be useful for small spraying jobs on individual specimen plants or small collections of plants.

Alternatively, chemical concentrates are available as either a liquid or wettable powder that are mixed with water to make a solution of the chemical. In this instance the water acts as a carrier for the chemical and conveys the pesticide to the plant. In solution the chemical can be applied through anything from a small hand-held sprayer to a knapsack sprayer that compresses the solution, either directly by a pumping action or by the use of compressed air.

At this point, it must be remembered that solutions should not be made stronger than recommended by the chemical manufacturer, as leaf scorching can quite easily result. Scorched leaves can also occur on plants that are sprayed in full sunlight when the spray droplets act as tiny magnifying lenses that concentrate the sun's rays resulting in the leaves or flowers becoming burned.

Spraying plants that are dry at the root is also dangerous for the same reason of causing possible scorch and should be avoided by ensuring that plants to be treated are moist at the root before treatment. This is especially important for container-grown plants that are particularly prone to this type of damage.

Not all spray solutions will effectively cover a plant's foliage adequately, or will stick to the foliage. This is due to either the waxy or downy nature of the foliage. For this reason the use of a wetting agent or surfactant can be particularly useful, as this breaks down the surface tension of the solution and helps to ensure a more even coverage of the leaf surface area. Fortunately, as some spray solutions are based on a soap solution, the material benefits from having a natural wetting action. However, if you are in doubt it may mean that you have to spray several times to gain control of a pest, due to the difficulty of applying an adequate volume of the poison to effectively give coverage of the plant and its unwelcome guests. Alternatively, the addition of soft liquid soap may be included to act as a wetting agent to increase the likely level of coverage and control.

When spraying, it is worth not only taking note of the plant's condition, but also the weather, especially for plants grown outside. Bright sunlight can as mentioned previously result in moderate to severe scorching. Wind can also be a nuisance, as it can reduce the effectiveness of coverage, as well as increasing the problems of spray drift. This can mean that the chemical is carried away from the plants being treated to other areas or plants that you may not wish to treat. Apart from any spray drift that could waft over the person spraying, the poison could cause immense damage to wildlife, especially if the drift contaminates ponds. For this reason, spraying is best carried out in calm conditions and never when it is windy. Also don't spray during or just before wet weather as the chemical will be washed off before it has time to take effect.

Aerosols

Another method of applying a chemical spray is by the use of an already formulated aerosol. This provides an ultra-fine mist of chemical spray in tiny droplets using a gas as a propellant and carrier. For essential environmental reasons take great care to ensure that any aerosol you select does not contain CFCs (chlorofluorocarbons), as these are known to be extremely damaging to the earth's ozone layer, allowing harmful ultra-violet rays from the sun to penetrate the atmosphere at a higher level. Before purchasing any aerosol, check that it is environment-friendly. Happily CFCs are being phased out, although stocks of aerosols containing the chemical may be around for a while yet. If you have doubts about an aerosol that you are thinking about buying, consider resorting to a mister or hand-held sprayer to apply the chemical instead.

Aerosols can however be particularly effective for small spraying jobs, where the tiny droplets carried by the action of the aerosol can penetrate the foliage cover quite effectively, sometimes more than a conventional spray. Unlike a conventional spray, which should be applied to run-off when the chemical droplets start to run together and drip off of the leaves, the application of an aerosol should be far more delicate.

The aerosol should simply be applied until such time as the plant has been covered by the fine mist, but not covered so heavily that you can see the spray collecting and building up on the leaves and certainly not to a run-off state. Applying an aerosol to excess can result in scorching, even if it is not applied in full sunlight. Flowers and young leaves are particularly susceptible to damage.

Dipping

A simple method of treating individual pot or container plants that are infested with an insect pest, can be by dipping the entire plant in a pesticide solution. Obviously, this can only be done when the plant is easily handled and is not too large to be immersed in a bucket or bowl of the solution.

This can however be a more wasteful answer to the problem of getting adequate coverage and control of a pest problem, due

Left:
A flexible pipe and lance help to improve access to a crop to improve coverage and control. Simply spraying over foliage is insufficient particularly when using organic chemicals, where thorough coverage is necessary. *Hozelock*

to the volume of pesticide solution required, as well as providing the user with a volume of surplus pesticide to safely dispose of. However, it can be a useful technique for treating a number of small plants when a sprayer is not available. In this instance, the pesticide solution is made up to the same strength as that recommended by the manufacturer as a spray solution

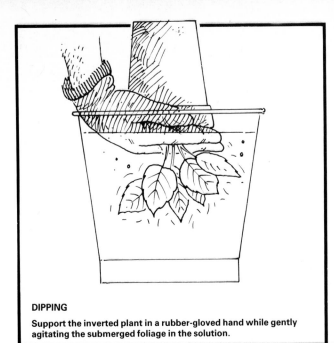

DIPPING

Support the inverted plant in a rubber-gloved hand while gently agitating the submerged foliage in the solution.

and is then thoroughly mixed to ensure that the solution is correctly prepared.

Each plant may then be inverted and carefully dipped in the solution, taking care not to submerge the plant's compost in the solution. Whilst the foliage is immersed, the plant should be gently agitated to move any air pockets and ensure that the solution is allowed to penetrate all parts of the plant's foliage. Once dipped and thoroughly wetted, remove the plant from the solution and gently shake it to remove any surplus pesticide, before being placed back in its original location.

Painting

When some pest problems are particularly localised on a plant, control can often be obtained by treatment of just the affected part. Pests such as mealy bugs can be treated effectively in this way. Take care though to ensure that you are not being too frugal and are not leaving any parts of the plant untreated that should be treated. Any pest will soon take advantage of this oversight.

To effect control, the pesticide solution can be simply brushed onto infested areas to wet the pest and hasten its doom. Apart from using anything ranging in size from a small artist's brush to a decorator's brush, very small areas can be treated with a cottonwool swab on the end of a matchstick.

Dusting

A further method of applying a pesticide can be by the use of a dust which is impregnated with chemical. This is usually available in a pack that can be squeezed to puff out the dust.

The technique avoids wetting the foliage, but does have a number of disadvantages. Firstly, it is a process that should only really be carried out in the open air, as the dust can spread in almost all directions. It can also be rather messy and can leave an unsightly deposit on the foliage, which can be a problem if the dust is used on plants with decorative foliage.

However, using a puffer pack to apply pesticidal dust to plants is quick, easy and very convenient, as there is no preparation or mixing of chemicals and the product is in a formulation that is ready to apply. To be effective, the dust should be applied in calm conditions and puffed evenly over, under and amongst the plant's foliage to obtain optimum coverage

Using an organic pesticide in a dust formulation requires care to ensure that maximum coverage is achieved and it is likely that repeated treatments will be necessary to effect total control.

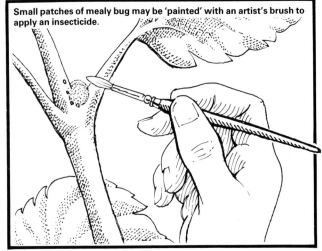

Small patches of mealy bug may be 'painted' with an artist's brush to apply an insecticide.

Smoke generators use smoke as a carrier for the insecticide and should only be used in a glasshouse. After fumigating open vents and doors and ventilate the glasshouse thoroughly.

As the treatment can be somewhat messy, it is probably advisable to only use a puffer treatment of a chemical dust for plants that are grown outside, although it could also be useful for pest control in a glasshouse.

However, remember that the dust can spoil the appearance of ornamental plants and unless the plants are growing outside, where rain will eventually wash off the chemical deposit, it is probably advisable to restrict its use to plants that will not be cosmetically spoiled.

Fumigation

Certain pesticides can be formulated into a smoke generator or cone, which can be quite effective for a rapid knockdown of insect pests infecting plants in a glasshouse, or to help control certain fungal diseases. Though these of course cannot be used outdoors or in the home.

The smoke formulation carries the chemical quite effectively throughout the glasshouse and permeates the foliage where the pest is poisoned by the material. Great care should be taken to ensure that the correct amount of smoke generators are used, as too little will probably be ineffectual and too much could easily cause damage.

It is also vital to ensure that plants are not dry at the root and are adequately moist. However, it is also important to ensure that the foliage is dry and that it is not to become exposed to the concentrated smoke by placing the smoke generator directly under plant foliage. Leaves that are wet will collect the particles of chemical from the smoke over the surface of the water droplets. As these dry, the chemical is concentrated on to a relatively small area of leaf and damage may subsequently result.

The use of smoke generators should be restricted to the glasshouse and should not be used in the conservatory, where the smoke could easily leak into the house.

As far as timing this treatment is concerned, it is certainly important not to carry out the procedure in sunlight, which is the normal precaution for the application of most chemicals. However, with a smoke formulation it is best carried out during the evening, when the glasshouse can be safely shut down and vents closed until morning. The glasshouse should then be adequately ventilated before entering. This gives sufficient time for the treatment to work, whilst minimising any likelihood of damage to plants or beneficial visiting insects such as bees.

Drenching

Not all pests are easily visible, indeed some are only evident when plants are dug up or removed from the pot. Pests such as root mealy bugs are a case in point and their presence can easily be overlooked until the loss of vigour and leaf yellowing of the infested plant encourages closer inspection to find the reason for the problem.

All other treatments previously mentioned will have little if any effect on soil-borne pests and to effect control a different type of method is required to expose the pest to an insecticide. In this instance, a drench treatment may be considered under certain circumstances. Water is used as the carrier and the pesticide is usually made up to a solution similar to that used for spraying. The compost in the pot, or for that matter the immediate soil around the plant in the garden, is then watered with the solution which should be applied evenly to ensure satisfactory coverage.

When applying a drench to a container-grown plant, apply slowly and evenly over the surface of the compost using a watering can with the rose removed. Surplus chemical should be collected in a saucer or drip tray underneath and then safely disposed of.

Applying a drench solution to plants growing out of doors, when they are growing directly in garden soil, requires a slightly different approach. In this instance the chemical solution should be applied from a watering can through a fine rose, in order to provide a thorough, but even application of the material. Applying the chemical solution slowly and carefully will help provide a balanced application and assimilation of the material.

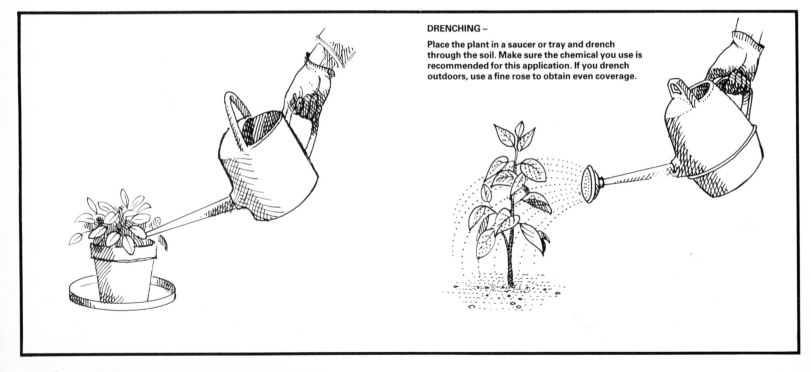

DRENCHING –

Place the plant in a saucer or tray and drench through the soil. Make sure the chemical you use is recommended for this application. If you drench outdoors, use a fine rose to obtain even coverage.

Timing of application

Never apply any chemical treatment in full sun, as scorching of the foliage can easily result. Conversely, it is obviously sensible not to apply a pesticide just prior to rain, or when rain is expected, as the material can be quickly washed away before it has had sufficient time to be effective.

The ideal time to apply a pesticide is either in overcast conditions, or during the evening. The evening is definitely preferable, as even organic chemicals can be lethal to bees and other beneficial insects. One should therefore wait until bees have finished their foraging activities for the day and have returned to the hive before any treatments are undertaken.

Any plant that requires treatment should be turgid and in no circumstances should a plant that is flaccid, ie wilting, be treated. The compost, or garden soil, should be moist and if it is dry it should be carefully wetted prior to treatment. Care should be taken to ensure that no water droplets are on any foliage that will be exposed to fumigation or dust.

In all cases never exceed the pesticide manufacturer's recommendations, but abide by them rigidly. Even organic chemicals can be phytotoxic, or in other words can damage plants, if they are used in excess or contrary to the chemical manufacturer's recommendations.

The frequency of application will again to some degree be governed by the pesticide manufacturer's advice, but will also be subject to the life cycle of the pest. It depends very much on whether or not the pest becomes sexually mature quickly after emergence, as to whether the pesticide should be applied as much as every few days, or only once every two weeks or so. The time of year and ambient temperature also affect this, as insect and other pest life cycles speed up at the height of summer and slow down dramatically later in the year, or when the weather is cooler.

Resistance

Resistance to pesticides is a more common problem of inorganic pesticides, which can not only be a nuisance, but also a considerable problem. It is always advisable to rotate the use of pesticides to ensure that the same chemical is not used too often, just in case its careless over-use could give rise to the possibility of resistance occurring, no matter how unlikely it is with organic chemicals.

A useful technique to avoid this build-up is to design a programme for pest control or prevention that incorporates a change of chemical used halfway or so through the programme,

Left:
Spraying tomatoes in the greenhouse — make sure you wait until evening so that bees have returned to their hives. Immense damage can be caused to beneficial insects by bad timing of pest and disease control. *Turbair Ltd*

to break the routine and check any potential problem. However, it has to be said that problems in controlling insect pests with organic pesticides are most unlikely to initiate a resistance problem.

When resistance to man-made pesticides does occur, it can present a real problem. Not only does the pests' resistance tend to be associated with the particular chemical, but also related chemicals from the same family as well. For example, resistance to an organo-phosphorous insecticide, such as malathion, may mean that the pest can also be resistant, or develop resistance to other organo-phosphorous chemicals as well. The same applies to chemicals within the same family, such as organo-chlorines, where similar levels of resistance can build up.

In all cases, resistance occurs when a chemical is used over a prolonged and repetitive period. This encourages the selection of pests, or for that matter strains of disease, that develop resistance or are resistant to the material. It also enhances this development by removing what would otherwise be competition in the form of other pests or disease organisms.

Treating with a sub-lethal dose, or amount of chemical less than what is effectively toxic, can produce a similar effect. It is therefore imperative that chemicals are used at the correct recommended rates and are applied thoroughly and consistently, with occasional variation in the spraying programme.

Prevention or cure?

Although a strong case could be argued for the use of pesticides only when they are really required and for them not to be used too indiscriminately, occasionally the case for preventative treatments should be considered.

Most often, pests are treated as and when they are seen. When this happens, they are usually noticed when it is almost too late and the plant has been severely damaged by a heavy pest attack. The long process to control the pest or disease ensues, requiring regular treatment until the problem has been eliminated.

In certain circumstances it is worth considering spraying, even before a pest or disease has become apparent, to prevent trouble from starting. This type of treatment is known as preventative, or prophylactic treatment and is particularly worthwhile for plants that are known to be susceptible to specific pest or disease problems at certain times of the year.

For example, the Blue Spruce (*Picea pungens* 'Hoopsii', P.P. 'Koster' or similar varieties) is particularly susceptible to aphids in the spring, which can severely damage the plant even before the plant appears to be badly affected. Needles are badly discoloured and damaged and are then rapidly shed by the plant, resulting in a visibly disfigured plant, which may take up to three or four years to grow over the damage, if ever it does. Quite often the gardener's patience evaporates and the plant is removed and disposed of. Similarly, the Alberta Spruce (*Picea glauca* 'Albertina Conica') is particularly prone to attack by red spider mites and suffers in much the same way as the Blue Spruce, except that the damage is almost always seen before the pest.

Aphids can at least be seen more easily, whereas red spider mites are very difficult to see with the naked eye and require close inspection with a magnifying lens to be adequately seen and identified. In both cases, the use of spray treatments every

Below:
Spray treatments applied early in the season can help to reduce potential pest problems. Some pests can cause great damage at even a low population, whilst rapid population growth of others can get out of control very quickly.

Left:
Even if preventative treatments are applied early in the season, it is important not to neglect repeat treatments and to allow pest problems to suddenly develop. Always regularly inspect plants for the earliest sign of symptoms of any problem.

two weeks or so in the spring to prevent the infestation occurring should be considered, as the cost of replacing one of these valuable conifers can be an expensive and upsetting experience.

If there is a golden rule to help decide whether or not to use such treatments, it perhaps should be that if a pest or disease problem regularly occurs at a particular time of year or under specific circumstances, such as following a prolonged dry spell, then it is worth considering preventative treatment. If a forecast or prediction cannot reasonably accurately be made, then resort to treating a problem when it is discovered, but keep a close check to ensure plants are regularly inspected.

3
Treatments or Deterrents?

It is imperative to note that organic does not mean 'safe', as indeed there are many inorganic pesticides that could be termed safer than organic materials. Nicotine for example is an extremely dangerous and poisonous product that requires very careful handling. It may be organic and therefore better for the environment, but it is very toxic and should be treated with the utmost caution and respect.

The range of organic pesticides available is not as extensive as the range of man-made products, which to some degree is rather a shame, as it does tend to limit the choice. It is also rather unfortunate that the spectrum of activity of organic pesticides is also not as diverse, which itself limits the ability to deal with insect pests in a truly comprehensive way.

However, the benefits of using organic products probably outweighs the disadvantages and problems. Many gardeners and horticulturists will gladly tolerate the lack of systemic activity, persistence or broad spectrum activity, knowing that organic products are safer for the environment. The concept of using organic products is based on the understanding that as they break down naturally, their by-products are unlikely to be damaging to the environment, with no risk of food chain poisoning or questionable decay or hazard from break-down products.

Not all of the chemicals mentioned are truly pesticides, in that they do not all kill pests. Some act as deterrents by helping to reduce the problem of a particular pest by attempting to keep it away in the first instance. This is usually achieved by a distasteful odour or unpalatable taste.

Alternatively, rather than using chemicals, even organic ones, a further method of control can be achieved by using biological control. Although closer control over the environment is an advantage and a level of pest infestation has to be tolerated to maintain a balance in order that the parasite or predator does not die off from lack of food, the benefits of biological control are clear. Firstly, no pesticides of any type are necessary and secondly, provided it is monitored correctly, the treatment should be an ongoing one that to some degree is self-perpetuating.

There is however one particular disadvantage that needs to be pointed out and that is what happens when another pest attacks a plant that is already being biologically treated for another pest. For example a plant that has red spider mite and is being controlled with the predatory mite Phytoseiulus may well become infested with aphids or whitefly. The idea of armies of parasitic and predatory insects and mites dealing with a myriad of pests might be attractive, but unfortunately is somewhat impractical.

Equally, great care needs to be taken when using biological control, for if one intends to eradicate another pest using an organic pesticide, it should be noted that the biological control could become invalidated as the pesticide kills off the beneficial insect or mite.

Apart from products that are truly organic or natural, having originated from a naturally occurring source, there are other products that are very closely related which one could perhaps describe as synthetic or man-made organics. Products such as allethrin, bio-resmethrin, permethrin, and tetramethrin are all related to pyrethrum, but have been modified and refined to produce a new generation of insecticides that have similarities to pyrethrum. However, they are nevertheless synthetic and the purist who wishes to abide by the absolute rules of organic gardening can be excused for not using these materials on the basis that they are no longer truly natural in the sense and meaning of the word.

This new generation of insecticides has a similar activity to pyrethrum and the products have similar benefits, in that they have low mammalian toxicity and a very high knock-down effect upon insects. They tend therefore to be extensively used where a low toxicity pesticide is required in areas such as public health.

Finally, a sobering thought, just because a chemical is organic does not mean that it is not a chemical by definition. Rotenone, often better known as derris, is described chemically as tetrahydro-dimethoxy-methylethemyl benzopyrano-furo-benzopyran-one! Pyrethrum and related pyrethrins are perhaps even more complex chemicals, albeit organic in nature.

Also, just because a chemical is organic does not mean that it does not damage the environment. Derris (rotenone) is exceptionally poisonous to fish and will cause great loss of life to fish stocks if it is allowed anywhere near garden ponds or watercourses. However, in the course of time it can be termed safer as its level of persistence is relatively short, thus making its longer-term impact upon the environment fairly minimal, providing it is used with care and consideration. Nevertheless it is essential to consider the environmental issues of careless use or disposal of organic pesticides and never to abuse them.

Finally, it is illegal to use chemicals that are not approved by the Ministry of Agriculture, Fisheries and Food, or to use any 'brews' or mixtures even from an organic origin that are again not approved for use.

The following range of products have been recognised to be useful for the control of pests and diseases. These products represent a relatively limited range of environmentally-friendly substances that are acceptable when practising organic gardening techniques. Nevertheless as regulations change and are often updated, always check to ensure that their use is recommended and do not use them if not.

Above:
A range of organic insecticide treatments. Such is the interest in these materials that the range now available is really quite comprehensive. *Koppert*

Aluminium sulphate

Aluminium sulphate, sometimes referred to as alum, can be quite effective in controlling slugs and snails, although it is not organic. A white crystalline substance, which is dissolved in water and sprayed or watered on to or around plants which are susceptible to the pests. Care should of course be taken, as damage may occur in the form of scorching, particularly when applied to dry plants.

Alum is considered harmless to birds, earthworms, hedgehogs and pets, when used as directed and works by making the slime-producing organs of slugs and snails contract.

The chemical is quite acidic and if watered onto the soil in excess, the pH or level of acidity in the soil can be lowered, ie made more acidic. This effect can be particularly useful when growing acid-loving plants such as hydrangea. For this reason, aluminium sulphate is sometimes sold as a hydrangea 'colourant'. Blue hydrangeas often produce pink flowers, when grown in conditions where the soil is less acidic and more neutral, or even alkaline. The effect of aluminium sulphate in lowering the pH helps the hydrangea to produce blue flowers. Failure to use the right amount of aluminium sulphate may result in somewhat muddy colours or a mixture varying from dull pink to purple.

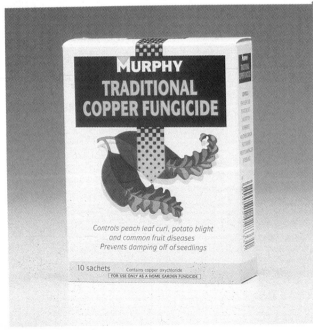

Copper

The use of copper as a fungicide has proved to be very effective over a number of years. Formulations used organically are Bordeaux mixture and Burgundy mixture. Bordeaux mixture is a well known and much used fungicide consisting of copper sulphate and quicklime, which has been used for many years for the control of a number of fungal disease problems.

Applied as a spray, Bordeaux mixture was initially formulated from a mixture of copper sulphate and calcium oxide (quicklime), but was later prepared from copper sulphate and calcium dihydroxide. The material needs to be agitated well and constantly in the water to ensure an even application and avoidance of precipitation in the spray tank.

The spray leaves a bluish tinge to the foliage that it is applied to and it was this characteristic that probably led to its discovery by a Frenchman, Alexis Millardet, who in 1882 was walking amongst the Medoc vineyards in the wine country of Bordeaux, when he noticed a strange difference in the vines. The vines close to the path where he walked still retained their leaves, whilst those well away from the path had defoliated. He also noticed that the foliage on the vines still in leaf had a faint blue coloration, or deposit on the surface, which he later found was a mixture of copper sulphate and lime applied to vines that grew close to the path to make them unpalatable to casual passers-by.

From this early attempt to discourage people from eating the grapes. Alexis Millardet started trials to improve the formulation to control the scourge of the vines, vine mildew fungus. In 1885 after three years of trials, he had mastered the formulation and proved that the material controlled vine mildew fungus by preventing the spores of the fungus penetrating the leaves. A further three years passed and in 1888 over five million acres of French vineyards were treated with the material, followed shortly after by the treatment of vineyards in America to control American black rot fungus and potato blight in France.

Apart from its activity, particularly as a protectant fungicide, Bordeaux mixture also has some bactericidal benefits as well as some minor acaricidal effects. However, its benefits may sometimes be outweighed to some degree by the fact that it can be quite phytotoxic, causing scorching and spotting of leaves and foliage, as well as being toxic to beneficial predatory mites.

Burgundy mixture is composed of a mixture of copper sulphate and washing soda and can be considerably phytotoxic to any foliage that it is allowed to come into contact with. Apart from being a fungicide that should be used with the greatest care, because of its propensity to damage the foliage of plants, Burgundy mixture can be used as a winter wash to help control disease spores. As with Bordeaux mixture, Burgundy mixture should not be mixed or stored in a metal container as it can actually start to 'plate' the surface with a fine film of copper. For this reason a plastic container is most useful.

Diatomaceous earth

This most unusual product is perhaps one of the strangest products for use as an organic insecticide. It is now rarely used as a pesticide, although its use to control weevils and beetles has enabled the product to be used not only on stored grain, but also on plants, livestock and in the home. Its use in organic pest control has mostly been in seed and grain storage, where it is formulated as a wettable powder, ie a powder that can be wetted sufficiently to produce a solution to spray.

Diatomaceous earth originates from various parts of the world, where it forms a deposit of sediment consisting of the fossilised remains of diatoms. Diatoms are single-celled plants that are microscopic in size of which there are believed to be something over 10,000 different species. These organisms are a class of algae with a cell wall that consists mostly of silica, which is why diatomaceous earth comprises approximately 80% silica-dioxide (SiO_2) as the main constituent.

The diatoms forming the product are not recent in origin, as they were fossilised probably in the tertiary period in seas and lakes many millions of years ago, where they formed a sedimentary deposit. These deposits, which are usually pale grey-green in colour and are crumbly and porous in nature, are found in the United States of America, Czechoslovakia and Germany.

Apart from use as an organic insecticide, diatomaceous earth has a most surprising range of uses. It is used as a fine grade powder with abrasive qualities and as a medium for filtering other products. Its use in paints to prevent rotting and as an insulator for boilers can only be superseded in its range of unusual applications by its use as a constituent of dynamite. This latter must not lead the reader to believe that insect problems are controlled by the product's use as an ingredient of an explosive to eradicate the pest! It is by the insecticidal properties of this unusual product that it provides a benefit as an organic insecticide.

Formaldehyde

Formaldehyde is rarely used in organic gardening these days, for although it is a very effective chemical, it is nevertheless somewhat limited in its range of uses. It tends to be used in horticulture now more as a sterilant than for its previous use in seed treatment, as damage to the seed can often occur.

The chemical was first used as a disinfectant in 1888 by Loew. In 1896 Geuther introduced its use as a seed disinfectant to help control seed-borne pathogens. The chemical is obtained by the oxidation of methyl alcohol using atmospheric oxygen and either copper or silver as a catalyst. The resultant chemical has an extremely strong, unpleasant and exceptionally irritating smell. As a liquid, formalin is colourless and is soluble in water and alcohol and contains 40% formaldehyde.

Formaldehyde has been widely used in commercial horticulture for seed treatment, soil fumigation and the fumigation of glasshouses. This latter use is carried out after the crop has been harvested and removed, prior to the following crop being introduced. It is a very strong and powerful antiseptic, deodoriser and disinfectant.

Apart from its application in the preservation of biological and anatomical specimens, a use that gives the biology department in schools and colleges their characteristic smell, formaldehyde is used in the manufacture of plastics, dyestuffs and in the tanning of leather. The material on being oxidised forms formic acid, the well known poison used by insects such as ants with great effect.

Formaldehyde is not at all a pleasant material to use and you should consider very carefully the problems of its handling and use. Even restricted to glasshouses as it is now, the very powerful and extremely distressing irritant effect caused by the very pungent odour is sufficient to put off the most enthusiastic and seasoned gardener.

Lime sulphur

Lime sulphur is used less often now than it used to be, but it continues to be effective as a preventative fungicide and also for some limited insecticidal use. In common with several other chemicals that have been used in organic plant care, lime sulphur was discovered to have fungicidal properties as long ago as 1886, when it was proved to be effective against a variety of scale insects by Dusey.

The product consists of a solution of calcium polysulphides and is manufactured by the solution of sulphur in a calcium hydroxide solution.

Although lime sulphur can be used in the summer and winter, the material is particularly popular as a winter wash to reduce and in some cases prevent the spread of disease and over-wintering pests. Care however should be taken when plants are in full leaf as damage can easily occur. A particular problem can occur with plants that are susceptible to sulphur, a reaction that is termed 'sulphur-shyness'. Varieties of fruit that are known to be susceptible are Doyenne de Comice, William and Louis Bonne of Jersey pears, as well as Cox's Orange Pippin, Beauty of Bath, Bismarck, Worcester Pearmain, Lord Derby and James Grieve apples. When dealing with fruit to control such problems as scab, it is better to spray early in the season in February or March.

Certain insect pests are also susceptible to lime sulphur. Red spider, big bud and some other mites can be reasonably controlled, as can woolly aphids and certain other aphids and scale insects, which were the first pests known to be controlled by the chemical at the end of the 19th century.

Lime sulphur can also be used to control mildew, leaf curl, black spot and cane spot.

It has been found that as the chemical breaks down, the residue of sulphur acts as a preventative fungicide giving the chemical a more interesting and broader spectrum of activity. It is also believed that lime sulphur actually has an effect of softening the protective wax coating on insect scales.

Nicotine

Nicotine is an extremely unpleasant and very toxic poison that needs to be treated with the greatest care. It is available but it is very potent and consequently most organic gardeners won't use it. The product is derived from alkaloids obtained from the leaves of the Nicotiana plant, which can contain anything from 1% to 15% of the poison. Apart from being extracted chemically from the leaves, the nicotine can be extracted by being distilled using steam. The nicotine is normally obtained from the leaves of *Nicotiana rustica* or *N. tabacum* and is a highly effective insecticide, even though its persistence is very short.

Although its 'life' after application is relatively short, manufacturers recommend a 48-hour interval between spraying and harvest and at least 12 hours before access is allowed to the crop.

The insecticide is a contact material and has been found to have some ovicidal (egg-killing) properties. It is particularly active against sucking and biting insects and can be applied in various ways to plants. Although more commonly available as a liquid formulation, it is also sometimes formulated into a dust or into nicotine 'shreds' for glasshouse fumigation.

The latter was a popular method of pest control under commercial glass and although it may be tried in a glasshouse well away from a dwelling or livestock, it should never ever be used in a conservatory. Great care should be taken with the process of fumigation, as the nicotine is impregnated in either cloth-like strips or paper pieces, both of which can readily burn rather than smoulder as they should, once lit. The paper formulation is certainly more likely to catch fire and apart from being a major fire hazard, particularly to a wooden structure, the effect of the fumigant is obviously wasted.

In whichever formulation that is chosen, greatest care should be taken when handling the product and protective clothing must be used, in particular a strong pair of industrial gloves. Nicotine is not just poisonous by being ingested, but is also very toxic by dermal (skin) exposure. Any fumes must also be avoided as it is also very toxic by inhalation.

The effect of the poison is to initially stimulate and then to paralyse the nerve ganglions, the parts of the nervous system that are receptors and transmitters of messages through the body. In many respects, the effects of the poison can be compared to another well known poison called curare, itself a poison of organic origin.

Nicotine also acts upon the body's digestive system by initially stimulating the salivary glands and then causing intestinal paralysis. A further problem occurs by its effect upon the heart by reducing blood pressure dramatically. Obviously any of the effects, or a combination of them will prove fatal if the amount ingested, inhaled or absorbed is high enough and illustrates why the material should be treated with the utmost care.

It is well known that as a drug in smaller quantities nicotine is addictive, as it is also known that workers in the tobacco industry have been known to suffer poisoning from handling the leaves and substances of the plant. At one time it was recommended to obtain the nicotine by soaking cigarette ends (obviously not filter-tipped ones!) and using the resultant solution, but this should not be done as there is little if any control over the strength of the solution obtained.

Although nicotine is very poisonous, it does have one thing in its favour and that is that it has a relatively short life. This means that if it is applied with care in the evening, when bees have returned to their hive, there should be much less danger to the bees by the time that they start to forage again the following morning. However most organic gardeners will not use it due to its high level of toxicity and you are best advised not to use it for this reason.

Pyrethrum

Of all the insecticides of an organic nature, it is probably pyrethrum that is the best known and most popular in use. However, it is not just one compound that is the only form in

use, as there are a number of pyrethrins used for their insecticidal properties.

Pyrethrins have been known for many years, having been exported from western Asia to Europe at some time around 1820. Imported as the dried flower heads of the white chrysanthemum-like flowered *Chrysanthemum cinerariaefolium* (sometimes called *Pyrethrum cinerariaefolium*), the insecticidal properties have proved of great value. Pyrethrins are also found to a lesser degree in the flowers of the red-flowered *Chrysanthemum coccineum* (syn *Pyrethrum roseum*) which are native of Caucasus. However, most of the pyrethrins are now imported from Ecuador, Kenya and Tanzania, from where something of the order of well over 20,000 tonnes are exported per annum.

Having been carefully dried, the resultant desiccated flower heads are then finely ground to a powder, which is then made into a dust or liquid formulation. Although very unstable in light, exposure to which destroys the insecticidal properties of the

Above:
Pyrethrum is an excellent broad spectrum organic insecticide. It is widely used in domestic, veterinary, industrial and public health situations as well as in horticulture.
Chase Organics Ltd

Left:
Ready mixed formulations are available in hand spray misters that are ideal for small spraying operations. This saves measuring and mixing up chemical solutions.

material and breaks down the product, pyrethrum is truly an amazing insecticide. Pyrethrins have a very low level of toxicity to mammals and although it may sometimes cause a rash, or other irritant effect, it is generally considered to be one of the safest, if not the safest organic insecticide.

Pyrethrins have very little effect on mammals, including man. When carefully prepared, the refined materials may actually lose any irritant effects, without affecting the efficacy of the product, due to the loss of the compounds that cause the problem. Pyrethrins are however very toxic as insecticides when a synergist is added, even though their effect is restricted to contact activity, without any systemic effect.

The material is particularly valued for its rapid knock-down results, coming from the paralysing effects of pyrethrins. It is however a chemical that has a short life due to the degrading effect of light upon the material. It should therefore be applied in dull conditions and preferably in the evening when its activity may last a little longer and when its damaging effects upon bees can be minimised by spraying after they have returned to their hives.

Apart from being highly effective against flying insects, pyrethrum is very active in controlling aphids, beetles, caterpillars, flies, weevils and whiteflies. Its life however is very short and may last approximately 12 hours. A disadvantage of the chemical is that it can sometimes taint food crops, although it is generally considered to be one of the safest and most desirable for such use.

Pyrethrins are also extremely useful insecticides for controlling pests such as fleas on domestic pets and for controlling household pests such as flies. Pyrethrum is widely used in the food industry both in its manufacture and preparation, where it is used to control flies and other insects that could contaminate foodstuffs.

Great care should be taken to ensure that pyrethrins are never used anywhere near fish, as pyrethrins are extremely toxic to fish. Even an aerosol sprayed briefly in the home can prove to be fatal to fish in an aquarium.

To ensure that the product used is totally organic, choose a formulation of pyrethrins that does not contain such synergists as *piperonyl butoxide*. These are 'artificial' chemicals added to enhance the activity of the product. These are particularly common in spray aerosol formulations, where it has to be said that the addition of piperonyl butoxide increases the level of insecticidal activity.

Many synthetic pyrethrins have been formulated including resmethrin, bio-resmethrin, permethrin and tetramethrin, each of which it has to be acknowledged have particular benefits, but may be frowned upon by the organic gardener.

Quassia

Quassia is a somewhat unusual insecticide, which is derived from wood chips from a tree called *Picrasma quassioides*. Quassia extract is a reasonably effective insecticide, although in comparison with some other organic materials it tends to be somewhat less efficient and tends not to be particularly active against beetles and caterpillars.

Historically, quassia extract was not only used to control infestations of head lice in children, but was also used domestically on flypapers before DDT regretfully appeared on the scene.

Unfortunately, quassia is not now so readily found as it used to be when it was freely available from chemists' shops. It is more commonly produced now as the concentrated extract which is a more intensified solution made from the wood chips of the plant. This is then diluted according to the manufacturers' instructions for spray application.

Quassia is active against aphids and has some level of activity against small caterpillars such as sawfly caterpillars. Also leaf mites, mites, red spider mites, scale insects and weevils. Fortunately, one of the benefits of its relatively low level of toxicity is that beneficial insects such as bees appear not to be harmed by the chemical. Adult ladybird beetles are usually unharmed, although the larvae may be affected. Generally speaking the larger and tougher the pests, the more difficult it is to control with quassia.

A further effect of quassia may be that it has some activity in deterring birds from damaging top fruit, due to the bitterness of the chemical on the surface of plants and fruits onto which it has been sprayed. Although this effect disappears as soon as it rains, as the material is very water-soluble, it may be that the chemical has a broader spectrum insect deterrent effect as well, whilst the chemical is in evidence. This level of bitterness can of course be a problem to the gardener for food plants onto which quassia has been sprayed. Such plants should be thoroughly washed after harvest before being consumed, as the chemical can taint food crops.

As with many organic insecticides, its level of activity is in direct relationship with the efficiency of spray coverage. This does not just mean applying a fine spray thoroughly over and under the foliage, as this may not be sufficient to satisfactorily 'wet' the foliage. Quassia extract is far more effective and active when combined in spray form with a surfactant or wetting agent such as soft soap. This helps to break down the surface tension of the solution and applies a more even 'film' of chemical solution over and under the surface of the plant tissue that is treated.

Rotenone

Rotenone is a useful and effective insecticide of organic origin that is particularly useful for its acaricidal (mite killing) properties. Its activity as an organic poison has been known for many years and was used by the Chinese as an insecticide and as a highly poisonous chemical that killed fish. Oddly enough, rotenone is also poisonous to pigs and tortoises and lacks the broad spectrum of safety benefits attributed to pyrethrum.

In other respects it shares some similarities to pyrethrum in that the main insecticidal ingredient, sometimes referred to as nicouline or yubatoxin, is broken down by light into products that have lesser effects. The chemical was first identified as a separate chemical by E. Geoffrey in 1895 and was formally analysed by E. B. Laforge in 1932.

The material is obtained from the roots of the plant *Derris elliptica*, giving rise to its other name of derris. Aker-tuba, derris root and tuba-root are other names for the root of the plant. The poison is also isolated from the roots of Lonchocarpus species, namely *Lonchocarpus nicou*, *L. urucu* and *L. utilis*, otherwise called barbasco, cube, haiari, nekoe and timbo.

As an insecticide, rotenone or derris has a low level of persistence in either dust or spray applications compared to most man-made insecticides, although it tends to be more persistent than pyrethrins. Rotenone can last for approximately 48 hours which can obviously be a problem when attempting to control insect pest problems when beneficial insects such as bees are around.

Although rotenone is not systemic and is purely a contact insecticide of a very low residual activity, it is a broad spectrum insecticide and kills a very wide range of pests such as ants, aphids, beetles, caterpillars, earwigs, mites, red spider mites, thrips and weevils. For this reason the benefit of being highly effective can also be a disadvantage, for the damage that it can cause to harmless insects. It should therefore be used only after due consideration, when the possible use of less damaging insecticides has been reviewed, in order to reduce the detrimental effects upon wildlife.

Great care should therefore be taken if bees are known to be foraging and its use questioned and substituted with an alternative chemical treatment if possible. Rotenone is also poisonous to other beneficial insects such as ladybird larvae. To minimise damage caused to helpful insects, it is important to consider spraying in the evening, as this may help to minimise the problems.

Formulations of rotenone are most commonly available as a dust or as a liquid. The dust normally consists of the dried and ground root mixed with an inert carrier to 'bulk up' the product.

Alternatively, the product is also available in a fairly concentrated liquid formulation, which when diluted can be applied as a spray.

Similar to pyrethrum, rotenone is a photo-chemical, ie it is degraded by light and care should be taken with its storage and use, particularly during sunny weather. To avoid reducing its efficacy, it is better to apply the chemical in dull or overcast conditions.

Below:
Rotenone or derris is a useful insecticide with acaricidal properties. It is however very toxic to fish and should be used with great care.
Chase Organics Ltd

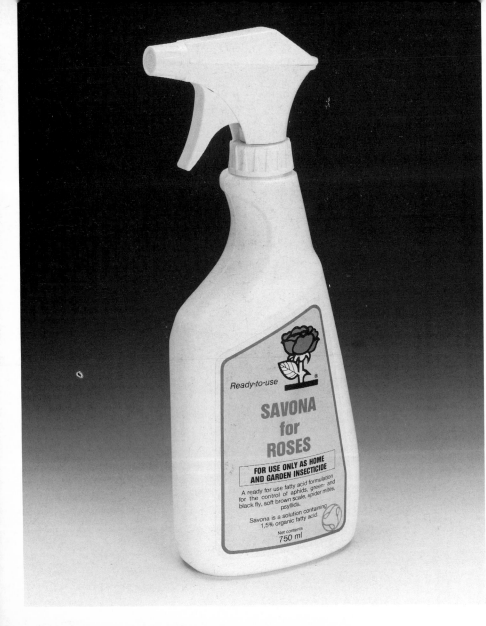

Ryanodine

Ryanodine, sometimes known as ryania, is an organic insecticide derived from the wooden stems of a shrub called *Ryania speciosa*. The wood is ground and the chemical is extracted and formulated into a liquid or powder product that can then be diluted for spraying.

Ryanodine is a relatively recent discovery and was first found to have insecticidal properties by B. E. Pepper and L. A. Carruth in 1945. The chemical was introduced later that year to the market as an insecticide.

Apart from being extracted from the stem wood of *Ryania speciosa*, ryanodine is also found in the leaves and roots of the plant. Once extracted from the ground plant material and crystallised, it has been found that the active ingredient, ryanodine, is up to 700 times more toxic than the actual plant material.

Ryania speciosa is a tropical shrub originating from South America and is found growing in the Amazon river basin and in Trinidad. The poison extracted from the plant is relatively low in its killing ability and is certainly surpassed by more active insecticides such as derris and pyrethrum. However, this fact is an advantage in certain circumstances.

Ryania or ryanodine has a mode of action that stops the insect from feeding, resulting in a much slower death than would be the case with pyrethrum or derris. Its selective activity as a stomach acting insecticide has the effect that certain pests such as codling moth caterpillars can be controlled, whilst others are unaffected. This can be beneficial if integrated pest control techniques are being used, for example when red spider mites are being controlled by the use of *Anthocoris nemorum*. This particular bug eats aphids, red spider eggs and mites and appears to be unaffected by ryanodine, whereas other organic insecticides can kill the bug.

However, despite the low level of toxicity and its somewhat selective activity, care should still be taken, for ryanodine is toxic to ladybird larvae, although apparently not to adult beetles.

Soap

The use of soft soap as an insecticide is probably one of the most common materials used to attempt to control aphids. Most older people, recalling their early years as a child in the garden, would almost certainly remember one of their parents or a neighbour, dowsing the roses with a bowl of washing water, or for the more sophisticated gardener, with the use of a hand syringe.

Although domestic soap is still often used, it is far better to use an industrial 'soft' soap. Domestic soap does work to a degree, but industrial soap based on caustic potash, rather than caustic soda, tends to be more effective. As the next best thing to industrial soft soap, it is possible to use a solution made from the old-fashioned kitchen soap, which consists of very hard cakes of household soap. In this instance the hard soap can be softened and dissolved in gently-heated water. Carefully stir the mixture and when completely dissolved, remove the resultant solution from the heat and let it cool before being used.

Alternatively, soft soap containing fatty acids can be readily bought as a proprietary product specially formulated as a concentrate for dilution, or as a ready-to-use product for insecticidal use.

To improve the efficiency of the solution, it is advisable to use 'soft' water, or preferably rainwater, as the effect of the hardness of calcium in the tap water results in the breakdown of the chemicals in the solution and the precipitation of 'scum'. Failure to do this will result in a solution that is less effective as a surfactant or wetting agent and therefore may mean that a stronger solution might have to be used to make up for its loss of activity.

Apart from being used as a wetting agent to improve the 'stickability' and coverage of chemicals applied to plants, a soft soap solution has insecticidal properties of its own. Used as a wetting agent, soft soap has quite often been mixed with nicotine, quassia extract and other materials to improve the effectiveness of the chemicals by helping to break down the surface tension of the solution. This helps to ensure that an even coverage of the chemical is applied over the surface area of the plant to which it is sprayed onto.

Applied on its own, when used in its own right as an insecticide, a solution of soft soap can be a reasonably good control for aphids (greenfly). Soft soap tends to cover aphids and act partly as a desiccant and partly as a suffocant. Aphids are covered with a thin waxy cuticle (skin) which is damaged by the soapy solution, resulting in the aphid desiccating (drying out) and suffocating by blocking the breathing pores in their skin.

As aphids are softer than bees, hoverflies and ladybirds, these beneficial insects are usually unharmed by the use of a soft soap solution, which is a further benefit of its use.

Soft soap is normally made from fatty substances obtained from plants and animals and unlike man-made detergents, is not derived from petrochemicals. These fatty acids can be bought in proprietary products, such as Savona, specifically as an insecticide.

Sulphur

Sulphur has been used as a pesticide for very many years and continues to enjoy a place amongst even the most sophisticated pesticides in use today. It is most commonly available in a form called 'Flowers of Sulphur', so called because of the shape of the crystals when examined in detail. It is also available as 'Yellow Sulphur' with a different crystal shape. This is considered by many to be less effective than flowers of sulphur, even though the chemical content is exactly the same and the only difference is the crystal structure.

Another formulation of sulphur is as a colloidal suspension. This consists of a very finely ground powder — sometimes called dispersible sulphur — that can be suspended in solution much more easily than other formulations, which can so easily precipitate out if mixed with water. The solution can then be applied as a spray.

Sulphur can be applied in various interesting and sometimes novel ways, the more interesting being limited to use in an enclosed environment such as a glasshouse. Apart from being formulated often as a dust to produce a material suitable for use in a puffer-pack, sulphur can also be vaporised.

Under glass, sulphur has been used extensively by rose growers to control mildew using a sulphur lamp. This heats the sulphur and vaporises it into the glasshouse atmosphere. Crystals of sulphur can often be seen 'growing' on obstacles above the heated bowl of the vaporiser. Another form of sulphur lamp heated the sulphur and combined the vapour with steam as a carrier to spread the sulphur evenly amongst the crop.

Great care always needs to be taken of course when heating sulphur, as it melts at 115°C and becomes fluid-like at around 160°C. Greatest care should always be taken not to ignite the material as sulphur forms poisonous sulphur dioxide on being burned. Not only is this highly damaging to plants, but it is also very dangerous to people, pets and wildlife and should not be inhaled under any circumstances.

Sulphur is generally a useful pesticide to be used for a large number of plants and is not usually phytotoxic (plant damaging), except to certain varieties of plants that are often termed sulphur-shy.

Its level of activity is normally confined to use as a fungicide, although it is known to have some acaricidal (mite-killing) properties. As a fungicide, sulphur has no systemic activity and works either by direct action upon the fungus, or as a preventative. When used as a protective treatment, the material's mode of action seems to be to inhibit or stop the growth of the fungal spores, due to the thin coating of the fine dust or powder on the surface of treated foliage.

4 Pest Deterrents

Pest control does not always mean that you have to eliminate the pest concerned, indeed if that was the case for most examples of biological control the ultimate result would almost certainly be disaster. It is therefore worth thinking about controlling pests by prevention, in other words attempting to keep them at bay and to try to avoid them gaining a damaging presence in the first instance. As can be imagined, this is not easy to achieve and if you decide to try it you must appreciate that the results are usually variable, almost never constant and sometimes unsuccessful.

However, if you want to avoid spraying or applying pesticides, even organic ones, then it may be worth trying some of these interesting and occasionally amusing techniques to deter pests from wreaking havoc amongst your treasured plants.

Although a subject in its own right, the use of plants to deter or attract insect pests is worth considering. The effect of plants upon each other may also have other interesting results. Some plants can promote improved growth and vigour in others and are known as 'companion' plants, whilst others can have an exactly opposite effect and can dramatically inhibit the rate of growth.

Berberis

The berberis is a shrub that is currently enjoying a new lease of interest, especially now that several recent new introductions in the form of more colourful varieties such as *Berberis stenophylla* 'Claret Cascade' and *Berberis stenophylla* 'Cream Showers' have appeared on the market. Apart from being a fine plant for the shrub border, the berberis makes a good low hedge, which in two or three years can deter dogs from breaking through and causing damage in the garden.

To help berberis thicken up its growth to provide a hedge that is less readily penetrated, lightly trim the wayward shoots after flowering. This will not only help to form the shape of the hedge, but will encourage more sideways growth to fill in any gaps.

The prickly nature of the hedge is a valuable asset in helping to deter unwanted dogs, or cats for that matter, but obvious care should be taken with it to avoid small children hurting themselves on the prickly leaves.

Birch

The common birch or silver birch is a very beautiful tree which graces most gardens where there is sufficient room for it. Provided it is planted some distance away from the house, the tree produces a beneficial effect, combining shimmering leaves with a gentle rustling sound in the breeze.

The birch's benefit in pest deterrence is that aphids love it and it may help to draw them away from other plants. However, be warned the penalty of this is that the invading population of aphids attacking the birch can build up to staggering proportions and even though natural enemies of the aphid take their toll of the pest, a great nuisance factor can develop. Not only can aphids eventually move on from the tree to find fresh feeding grounds, but also the wretched pests excrete the notoriously sticky and messy honeydew which drops on to other plants below spoiling their appearance, by making their leaves glossily sticky.

Birch trees close to a road or driveway will deposit a mass of sticky globules onto any vehicle left under it, even if left for only a few hours, with the result that the car with its new gluey finish attracts flies, wasps and dirt. Unfortunately, it can then be very difficult to clean.

On the positive side, for the keen conservationist a birch tree attracts quite a host of wildlife including small caterpillars and other insects, which in turn attract many birds including various members of the tit family which help to contribute towards some level of balance of nature.

Brassica collars

These simple collars act as a physical deterrent to cabbage root fly. Normally the insect would lay its eggs close to the plant's stem at soil level. However, the collar physically prevents this from happening and the frustrated insect has to search elsewhere for a site to lay its eggs.

Left:
The silver birch not only attracts a wide range of wildlife, especially birds, but almost acts like a 'magnet' to such insects as aphids. *K. March*

Far left:
Various new varieties of berberis are available that can be very effective as hedging that is both ornamental and also at deterring cats and dogs.
Blooms of Bressingham Ltd

Right:
The brassica collar is a simple device which can help to protect brassicas against cabbage root fly.

Camphor

Camphor is a very useful material for deterring a number of difficult pests in the garden and for that matter in the home as well. The material is a white crystalline chemical that occurs naturally in the sap of a plant called *Cinnamamon camphora*, or perhaps more commonly the camphor plant or tree.

The pleasantly pungent material is particularly good at helping to deter clothes moths in the home and is also a very good fly deterrent. Ants also dislike it and if applied too close to the nest the result may be fatal to them, which is a shame in most instances, as ants are beneficial in the garden. They can of course be a nuisance in the house when they appear indoors and start raiding the larder and forage around the house for food.

The keen gardener who takes pride in a beautifully kept lawn may be desperately frustrated by moles and might resort to all sorts of obscene methods of controlling them, including poison-baited earthworms, poison gas mole fuses or even mole traps, which although effective are nevertheless cruel. The pungent smell of camphor on the other hand provides a more humane deterrent, even if it only temporarily deters the mole from your lawn to your neighbour's lawn for a while!

Celery

Celery, apart from being a good salad vegetable, can help to keep cabbages in a healthier condition by deterring cabbage pests. However, celery in turn may nevertheless attract and be attacked by such pests as leaf miner, slugs and even carrot root fly.

Chamomile

The wild chamomile, *Matricaria chamomilla*, apart from having quite a pronounced smell, is used to deter onion fly from attacking onions and leeks. Try cultivating the plants close to the onions by growing them between the rows to help deter the pest concerned.

Chervil

Apart from being a relatively useful aphid deterrent, chervil can sometimes act as a moderately successful defence against slugs and snails, when grown close to susceptible plants.

Citronella Oil

The use of citronella oil which is derived from a South Asian grass not only deters gnats and flies, but is also very effective against cats and dogs. It is available impregnated into candles and as a liquid to spray.

Citrus

The use of various citrus extracts can be particularly useful for deterring some real nuisances in the garden and home. The oil of lemon will certainly deter flies and gnats and may be worth trying of a summer evening, when enjoying a barbecue or a garden party.

Another pest can be the domestic cat, especially when it scratches holes in newly sown seed beds to great detrimental effect. Bits of fresh orange peel cut carefully into roughly 2-4cm square pieces and scattered over seed beds can help to keep cats at a distance. Seeing a cat attempt to make its way amongst the orange peel can gladden the heart of a frustrated gardener as the cat quite often smells the strong citrus and shaking its paws and head quickly disappears to find another site.

Cress

Cultivating radishes as a salad crop can be frustrating, especially when flea beetles keep attacking them. Growing cress near the rows of radishes can assist the radish to grow a little less bothered as the flea beetles seem to prefer the cress, which they often attack instead. The method is hardly a deterrent, but may sometimes work by helping to minimise the damage.

Dill

Dill is another strongly aromatic herb that can sometimes deter aphids from attacking nearby plants when planted alongside. Similarly, dill can sometimes dissuade slugs and snails from attacking neighbouring plants.

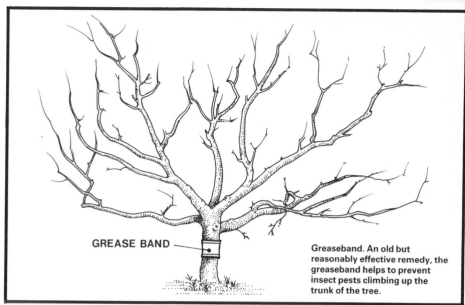

GREASE BAND

Greaseband. An old but reasonably effective remedy, the greaseband helps to prevent insect pests climbing up the trunk of the tree.

Garlic

Similar to onions, garlic seems to have deterrent qualities for certain types of aphid and some other insect pests. It is worth cultivating close to plants that suffer from such pests.

Greasebands

This old remedy is still useful in helping to control winter moth caterpillars, earwigs and other pests which would readily be able to climb up any plant or tree were it not for the greaseband. The mode of action is that of simply acting as a slippery barrier to the pests by preventing the insect from crossing the band.

Hawthorn

When planted as a hedge hawthorn forms an almost impenetrable barrier against dogs and cats coming into the garden. Within about three years, simple pruning to even out the growth encourages the plant to produce a reasonably compact, bushy habit. Regular trimming several times a year during the growing season will maintain the shape of the hedge and open spaces will quickly fill in to close any gaps. The hedge

Far Left:
Dill — strongly aromatic it can deter pests. *Chase Organics Ltd*

can also be laid by bending down branches to close off larger gaps, which it does very rapidly and effectively.

Hawthorn is a magnet for wildlife, not all of which is beneficial, and mildew can despoil the hedge from spring through the time when it is in leaf. Aphids and other sucking insects can dull and further damage the foliage, which is made all the more unsightly by the effects of sticky honeydew, the excrement of the pests, that encourages the growth of unsightly sooty mould. However, many beneficial insects also make hawthorn their home.

Although the hawthorn is hard to surpass for its 'stockproof' ability, care should be taken, as the thorns can be very nasty and dangerous especially to small children. Any scratches from the hedge should be quickly treated as wounds can rapidly become infected and turn septic.

Hedges that are not trimmed too vigorously will produce flowers that attract bees in the spring, followed by colourful berries (haws), which the birds consume with great pleasure in the autumn and winter.

Hyssop

Hyssop officinalis is another plant which can benefit nearby plants by helping to minimise aphid, slug and snail attacks.

Lavender

No garden should be considered complete without lavender being grown somewhere in it. Apart from the attraction of the clumpy silver-grey foliage, the plant is at its best when it flowers at the height of summer. Not only does the plant attract a myriad of butterflies and bees, but it also helps to deter aphids, especially on nearby roses.

The scent of lavender can also help to deter moths in the home from damaging fabrics. Gnats may also be deterred from being a nuisance at night. In this instance the use of the lavender in its oil form might be found to be more effective.

Noise

Various pests can actually be effectively deterred by noise. Apart from the propane guns used by farmers that issue a retort similar in volume to a small item of artillery, which would not be popular with the neighbours, there are far more quiet and less drastic solutions to the problem of frightening away nuisance birds.

Strips of aluminium foil can be a useful scare device when hung from trees, branches or, perhaps better, from wires

Facing page, top:
Although hawthorn is deciduous and loses its leaves in the autumn, it produces a very effective hedge and barrier to cats and dogs. It can also be a very attractive host to an abundance of insects. *K. March*

Facing page, bottom:
Apart from being attractive to bees and other beneficial insects and useful in its own right as an ornamental garden plant, lavender can help to deter nuisance pests.

Left:
Pyracantha. The firethorn or pyracantha can be an effective screen and hedging plant with fierce thorns. It is however particularly attractive when in flower or later in the year when the colourful berries are produced.

supported on a frame. Not only are birds deterred, but deer and rabbits may also react to this simple device.

A further product actually emits a 'hum' when it is suspended between posts. This tape or line can be quite effective in helping to keep birds away from newly sown seed beds.

Onions

Onions can be beneficial in helping to deter aphid attacks. When planted near to roses they also are supposed to increase the intensity of the scent of the rose, assuming of course that you can smell the roses above the pungent aroma of the onion and can tolerate the rather strange plant association. However, the ornamental onions — Alliums — are most attractive, and while not quite so pungent, can nevertheless be effective.

Pyracantha

Also called Firethorn, pyracantha is another good hedge plant that can produce a very effective boundary and barrier to cats and dogs. The thorns can be particularly long and dangerous and this fact must be carefully considered before planting the hedge, especially if one is considering planting close to a pathway or drive.

Similar to berberis, the plant should have any wayward branches lightly trimmed to maintain a more compact habit. If the right place can be found to cultivate the plant without danger to others, consider varieties such as *Pyracantha* 'Orange Glow' with vivid orange berries in late summer and autumn or P. *'Soleil D'Or'* which produces golden yellow berries.

Pyracantha is a good wildlife plant with white flowers that attract bees in the spring and berries which the birds enjoy in the autumn.

Rue

Not all plants need to sport a fiercesome array of thorns to deter dogs. Rue can help to put off dogs quite well by its presence when grown in strategic positions in the garden.

Sage

The common sage may help to deter aphids and to some degree slugs and snails, when planted close to susceptible plants.

Savory

Yet another herb that may help to deter aphids, slugs and snails.

Shallots

The smell of shallots can help to deter aphids in much the same way as the use of onions. They also help to deter carrot fly larvae in the soil.

Spring onions

Similar to shallots and onions, spring onions may help to not only deter aphids, but to also deter carrot fly larvae.

Stones

Small rough stones, grit, shingle and even broken eggshells help to form a reasonably effective barrier to slugs and snails. Although it is difficult to envisage an effective barrier all around the garden to act as a security prevention zone, with careful planning the use of such materials placed around such susceptible plants as hosta can help to prevent slugs and snails attacking the plants.

It is worth trying various materials to select the most effective, as this type of physical barrier is only worth using if the material has been proved to work in the garden concerned and that the barrier is unbroken and not too unsightly. Take care to also ensure that no leaves or branches from the susceptible plant arch over the barrier and make a bridge with the soil on the other side. Nearby plants can also allow passage to the plant if they make contact. The key is therefore careful isolation and constant attention to maintain the defences.

Straw-filled pots

Hardly a deterrent, small flower pots filled with straw and inverted on canes placed against dahlias and other susceptible plants help to reduce the problem of earwigs by attracting them.

The pots, measuring about 6-9cm (2½-3½in) offer a good hiding place for earwigs after their evening forage. The following morning remove the pots and dispose of the offending insects, then refill the pots with fresh straw and replace them for the next evening. Repeat the process every day until such time as the problem has been reduced to a minimum.

It looks unlikely but it really works! 6-9cm (2.5-3.5in) flower pots filled with straw and inverted on bamboo canes can trap earwigs.

Left:
Tagetes, the African or French Marigold encourages hover-flies — the scourge of the aphid.
Chase Organics Ltd

Tagetes

Tagetes patula, sometimes called the African or French Marigold gives off a very pungent smell from its foliage and more particularly from its flowers.

By attracting hover-flies to the flowers, the African or French Marigold encourages the hover-flies to breed and produce larvae which are particularly fond of aphids and have a voracious appetite for them. This can be extremely useful amongst such plants as roses, which most years will be infected throughout the spring and summer with greenfly, if not appropriately treated.

The tagetes also has another useful deterrent effect when grown amongst tomatoes and potatoes. Here it can actually help to deter soil-borne eelworm, which can be particularly damaging to the crops by the pest known as tomato cyst eelworm and potato cyst eelworm. Both can seriously damage the plants and drastically reduce the cropping potential. It is believed that the tagetes actually excretes substances from its roots which the eelworm find distasteful and thereby reduces the possibility of an infestation being as severe as it otherwise would be. Whether tagetes can actually provide complete protection may be hoping for rather a lot, and the level of success depends much on the density of planting and other factors such as rate of growth and health of the guard plants.

African or French Marigolds can also be useful in keeping ants away when they are found to be a nuisance. Although this may be somewhat unlikely in the flower beds or vegetable garden, the use of tagetes as a barrier plant to prevent ants entering the house may be found to be useful. Planted close to the house and particularly close to gaps in the mortar, doors, cracks or crevices, but not too close to any air bricks, the plant will help to prevent ants from entering the house and becoming a nuisance by foraging for food in the larder or around the kitchen.

Another pest which may be deterred is the whitefly, particularly as a pest on tomatoes. The pungent scent of the tagetes and the chemicals apparently released from the roots into the soil may well enable the tomato to benefit from being exposed to a material or materials that help to keep whitefly away. However, the smell of the leaves and flowers may also contribute to the deterrent effect.

Below:
Scaraweb — a useful barrier against birds.
Chase Organics Ltd

Thyme

This attractive and most useful, if perhaps diminutive, plant is a useful herb and can be an extremely effective plant for the rock garden.

Although thyme is supposed to deter aphids from attacking nearby plants and to act as a defence plant against slugs and snails, its effectiveness as far as slugs and snails must be treated with some scepticism. Alpine thymes in particular may actually disappear overnight due to the ravaging by slugs and snails. They may therefore be good plants to be sacrificed for other plants, or it is possible that certain varieties are more susceptible than others. The use of thyme against slugs and snails should therefore be considered and tried with care and perhaps a little suspicion.

Valerian

The use of valerian may well help to dissuade that most unwelcome and dreaded of pests in the garden, the rat.

The intensive smell of the plant not only may help to dissuade rats from coming near to the plants, but may also help to attract cats which appear to like the smell. Perhaps either effect may help to reduce the problem of this dreadful disease-ridden pest.

Wherever rats may be expected to enter the garden, such as from ditches, near compost heaps or outbuildings, it is worth planting *Valerian officinalis* and to hope that the idea works.

Webbing

More a physical barrier than a deterrent, there is a special type of fine rayon webbing available that can act as an extremely effective barrier to birds. The very fine netting is simply placed over soft fruit or top fruit (where not too large) and helps to prevent such birds as bullfinches, that can be quite devastating if allowed free access.

It is essential to use the right sort of webbing that the manufacturers advise so as not to trap and kill wild birds. Equally, it is important not to improvise with a material that could cause such unnecessary suffering.

Another interesting material is based on polypropylene, which is available as a fabric material called Agryll that can be placed over various plants. Not only can it improve growth by protecting plants against the elements, although allowing the easy transmission of essential light, water and air, it can also act as a physical barrier to pests. Apart from being an obvious barrier to birds, it can also deter aphids, cabbage root fly and carrot fly.

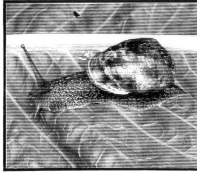

5 Biological Control

Without the intervention of human beings cultivating plants, often in a monoculture situation, nature generally manages to maintain some degree of natural balance. However, as plants are often grown in large numbers of the same variety, even in domestic gardens, it is so easy for this balance of natural control to be seriously disturbed. This is further compounded by the use of pesticides which indiscriminately kill beneficial insects as well as malevolent pests. It is also a fact that the countryside and domestic gardens are fast becoming sterile, sanitised areas that offer little cover for wildlife.

Vast acreages of farmland with little cover from trees and hedgerows are almost deserts as far as wildlife is concerned. Even close-cut grass parklands and gardens that are kept tidy to the point of excluding any weed or plant that dares show its presence, all offer little to encourage nature to do its bit.

In an ideal situation, nature creates a balance even if at times it does look as if it gets out of order when plagues of aphids appear. However, plants that grow healthily in balance are much less likely to be subject to pest and disease problems. Although part of the reason for this lies in the fact that the plants' health and strength contributes to its resistance, the other factor is that of the effects of beneficial insects, animals, fungi and even bacteria, which all do their bit to control pests and diseases.

For this approach to be successful, it is imperative to provide the right conditions for the organisms to thrive and not to kill them off by the careless use of pesticides, even organic ones. Equally, some study must be made of what these beneficial organisms require to over-winter where appropriate, otherwise pests and diseases can get quickly out of control in the early spring, before new control organisms can be introduced.

This method of control using natural predators and parasites is called biological control and it has to be said is not an easy technique to manage, with the exception of one or two specialised examples. For the technique to be successful, the gardener has to learn to accept the problem of managing the pest and its predator or parasite. This means having to accept

Below:
The ladybird larvae, like the adult, is a highly effective predator of aphids. Its voracious appetite for aphids is truly amazing. *Crown Copyright*

that for the technique to be 100% effective, that the predator or parasite as well as the pest is encouraged to live in balance.

Ideally, if you can accept the fact, biological control needs a continuing balance to be maintained. This further requires that one has to learn to tolerate a constant population of pests, or level of infestation, whilst at the same time hoping that the predator or parasite can maintain its own population in balance. Simply eliminating the pest results in the food source of the predator or parasite disappearing or running out, with the obvious effect that the beneficial organism dies or migrates because of lack of food.

It has to be stated that biological control is not easy to maintain totally effectively, as there are so many other factors that can disturb the natural balance. Amongst these are such elements as the competition of other beneficial insects together with birds, amphibians and other animals. A further complication lies with the vagaries of the weather, which quite often appears to detrimentally affect the predator or parasite before the pest.

Ideally, where you can have some control over the environment, the results of using biological control may be more promising. This is certainly likely to be most evident when controlling such pests as whitefly or red spider mites in a glasshouse or conservatory. Even then this technique may still not suit everyone, as you still have to accept a level of the pest to ensure that the technique continues in balance.

Sadly, the use of an integrated programme using organic pesticides and biological control is rarely successful, as organic pesticides are usually broad spectrum in their activity and will eradicate beneficial insects just as easily as the pest. This can be a particular problem when a pest is being controlled satisfactorily by biological methods until a further pest then attacks the plant. The difficult decision then has to be made whether or not to spray, with the risk of not only killing the pest, but destroying the biological control programme in the process. Alternatively you might be able to introduce another biological control factor, if there is one available. However, it has to be said that this is not easy and is very hard to effectively manage.

For those wishing to consider biological control, the following pests have been effectively controlled, although it must be stressed that the results will certainly vary according to the conditions experienced. Where predators or parasites are available commercially, this is preferred to relying on naturally-occurring biological control agents. With commercially available material one can at least top-up the level, whereas the amount of natural material will vary according to many factors and should therefore only really be relied on to assist control in most situations.

Aphids

Aphids have to be one of the most common pests of garden plants and crops grown outside and under protected cultivation. Fortunately, there are quite a number of natural predators and parasites that can help to reduce the population of this troublesome pest.

However, there are many different varieties of aphids, some of which have quite specific organisms that affect them. As with all methods of biological control, the importance of maintaining balance is imperative, as imprudent use of pesticides can

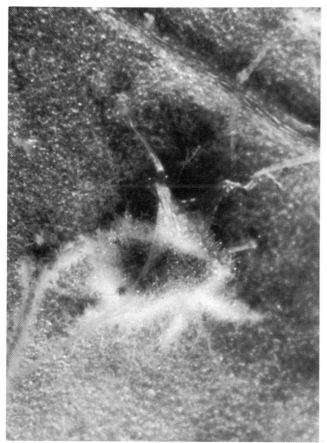

seriously disturb the natural balance, resulting in a dramatic recovery of an aphid population due to the lack of predators or parasites.

Amongst the naturally occurring predators, the most well known and effective must be the ladybird, of which there are also many different types. Not only are aphids attacked and eaten by the adult ladybird, but also the larvae, both of which have a voracious appetite for these fleshy, succulent pests. To see a ladybird in action can even make the hardest-hearted gardener feel some sympathy for the doomed aphid!

The delicate lacewing, so often seen at the end of the summer in the house, is another excellent predator of aphids, as are hover-flies. The larvae of both of these insects can again have a dramatic effect upon reducing the aphid population.

Many types of aphid are also attacked by fungi, which are particularly effective when the weather is humid and warm, when the fungus is most active. The fungus readily produces spores, which then rapidly infect other aphids throughout the colony. For the aphid that has wings and flies away to find new areas to feed upon there is also no escape, for not only are the spores carried by them to infect themselves, but also their offspring.

Another hazard faced by aphids is that of small parasitic wasps, which lay the eggs of their young directly within the bodies of the aphids. The effect of parasitisation is really quite horrific, for once the female wasp has laid her eggs inside the

Facing page, top:
Despite their delicate appearance, the lacewing enjoys a diet of aphids, and can be a particularly welcome predatory insect of a real nuisance pest. *Crown Copyright*

Facing page, bottom:
Hover-flies also play a valuable part in helping to control aphids, although they are difficult to encourage in number and really only complement the activities of ladybirds. *Crown Copyright*

Left:
Aphids can also be controlled by a parasitic fungus, which is occasionally seen and can help to reduce the population. *Crown Copyright*

Above:
A female parasitic wasp lays an egg in the body of an aphid, the aphid is now doomed as it is literally eaten alive. *Crown Copyright*

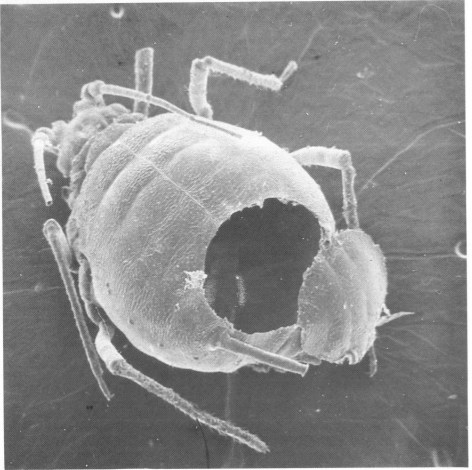

husk-like body at its back from a small round hole that it creates to make its escape. The newly-emerging parasite then repeats the process for successive generations of aphids.

Unfortunately, the parasitic wasp is not very hardy and only the mildest of winters favours the possibility of their survival and successful over-wintering. As the parasite prefers warmer conditions for its effective contribution towards helping to control aphids, its level of activity may be disappointingly low during a typical English summer when conditions can be cool and damp and are therefore unfavourable for the wasp.

Apart from these more diminutive predators and parasites, one should not forget the contribution made to controlling aphids by the wild bird population. Tits are especially very active in reducing the population of small insects such as aphids.

Caterpillars

Caterpillars can be a real nuisance to ornamental and food crops causing at the very least deformation of the foliage and at the worst almost a complete stripping of others. The voracious appetite of a caterpillar really has to be seen to be believed, if you can tolerate watching the effects upon your plants.

Tortrix moth caterpillars can be particularly difficult to control, as they tend to enclose themselves in leaves that are folded around them, held by the silk that they spin. Damage to younger leaves and flowers is most likely and leaves that appear to be stuck together may, once separated, expose the caterpillar feeding inside. A parasitic wasp, *Litomastix aretas,* the chalcid wasp, is an extremely potent parasite effecting a very high rate of control of the tortrix.

Other caterpillars may also be controlled naturally by parasites. The sawfly for example is often parasitised by a tachinid fly which lays its white eggs on the caterpillars. The eggs then hatch and the caterpillar suffers a most gruesome death by being eaten alive by the larvae of the fly.

Not all predators and parasites are small however, for some caterpillars such as winter moths may be predated upon by small mammals such as shrews — provided of course that the family cat does not biologically control the shrew first! Caterpillars and pupae may not only succumb to shrews and other creatures, but can also be parasitised by other hymenopterous parasites such as wasps and flies.

Apart from these naturally occurring control organisms, there are also two exceedingly effective biological measures. The first can loosely be described as being biological, whilst the second

young aphids, the eggs hatch and the larvae consume the inside of the aphids' bodies, prior to forming pupae inside the bodies of the dead aphids. Although the aphid is dead at this stage, it still continues to be attached to the plant.

During this process, the appearance of the parasitised aphid changes quite noticeably and takes on a darker, blackish hue once the stage of parasitisation becomes more advanced. The pupa then hatches and the parasite breaks out of the aphid's

certainly is. The former is probably less effective than the latter, but is certainly the easier of the two techniques to use. It simply involves the use of a trap which attracts the insects and catches them by sticking them to the core of the trap. This core is often replaceable and in some cases relies on the insect being attracted by the colour of the core.

However, by far the most ingenious involves the use of a pheromone, or sex scent, as it is sometimes described. Male moths in search of a female to mate with may be attracted over great distances to what they incorrectly believe is a female moth. Instead of fertilising the female moth, to produce offspring, the male is duped into wooing a man-made trap exuding the scent and is trapped. In the meantime, unless the female moth can attract a male who picks up her scent rather than that of the trap, she may well be deprived of a mate and is therefore unable to reproduce.

Above:
Pheremone traps are an effective method of controlling caterpillars by trapping male moths before they can mate with female moths.
Crown Copyright

Far right:
Red spider mite predators are simply sprinkled over the infested crop, they then feed on the pests and establish a population.

A further method, which is extremely effective at controlling many caterpillars, involves the use of a biological control spray. In some respects this somewhat sinister material, using the technology of germ warfare, may appear on first account to appear distasteful, but for the gardener plagued by caterpillars it is probably his or her best method of biological control.

The material consists of a bacteria, *Bacillus thuringiensis,* which is available in a powder formulation. Once mixed with water and sprayed onto the infested plants, the material works very quickly on the caterpillars. The bacteria has a devastating effect upon the caterpillars once it is ingested with the leaf tissue onto which it has been applied. Specific to caterpillars, the bacteria rapidly poisons the creature within a day or so. Poisoned caterpillars often appear to reduce quickly in size as the bacteria works upon the gut and they often take on a blackened appearance before finally shrivelling up and dying.

Fungal diseases

Surprisingly, there is even a way to help control some fungal disease problems by the use of a beneficial fungus. Although it is particularly of benefit for the control of *Chondrostereum purpureum* (Silver Leaf Disease) of top fruit such as almonds, apples, apricots, cherries and plums, the fungus can also help to prevent diseases entering through wounds.

The fungus called *Trichoderma viride* can either be applied as small pellets, which are placed in holes drilled in the tree, or can be made into a thick cream made from a powder mixed with water which can be painted with a brush on to wounded areas. Prior to treating in this way, the damaged area should be tidied up by sawing cleanly, or removing any damaged tissue with a sharp knife or pair of secateurs.

The material can also be made into a spray solution and whichever way used helps to prevent, as well as control fungal diseases by its parasitic effect upon other fungi.

Leaf miners

Leaf miners are as their name implies insects that tunnel within the leaf tissue. This activity renders them very difficult to control with organic contact insecticides. Commercially, they are partially controlled using systemic insecticides that are translocated within the plant.

Although to some degree a marginal level of control can be obtained by spraying to kill adults with an organic pesticide, the pest may also be controlled by the use of parasitic wasps which can parasitise the larvae of the leaf miner. Mature larvae are parasitised by a wasp called *Opius*, whilst the very young recently hatched larvae are parasitised by *Diglyphus*. Using both types of parasitic wasp will help to ensure that the population of leaf miners is kept at a minimal level.

Mites

Red spider mites or two-spotted spider mites are particularly problematic under glass in conservatories or glasshouses, where warm dry, sunny conditions favour their rapid spread. Unfortunately, they can be particularly difficult to control due to the fact that they prefer to live and feed on the undersides of leaves, making them more difficult to reach when spraying. Possibly for this reason biological and natural control measures offer particular benefits, as natural predators can be more effective at finding and controlling the pest.

The most commonly used commercial method of biological control under glass is *Phytoseiulus persimilis,* a predatory mite which is similar in size, although perhaps just a little bit larger, than the red spider mite or two-spotted spider mite. It is also much faster moving than the prey and runs around on the underside of the foliage in search of mites to attack and eat. The predators can be purchased in a small sachet and the contents are simply sprinkled onto the infested plants. The eggs of the predator hatch and the young predatory mites then search for their living food.

Apart from Phytoseiulus, which is probably only suitable as a control measure under glass, due to its preference for higher than ambient temperatures, a naturally occurring predator called *Typhlodromus pyri* can be quite effective in helping to reduce the numbers of the pest. Vying with typhlodromid mites for the level of efficiency in controlling spider mite pests is the anthocorid bug, which as a small beetle has other beneficial activity in controlling aphids.

Further control of mites may also be effected by other natural creatures such as *Stethorus punctillum,* a diminutive black ladybird beetle and *Oligota flavicornis,* a staphylinid beetle. There are even some species of thrips which, unlike the plant pests, can actually be useful predators of mites as well as types of mirid bugs, one of which being the black-kneed capsid, *Blepharidopterus angulatus.*

An essential point to remember, particularly with biological control of mites, is the need for adequate over-wintering accommodation of the predators. Unfortunately, the predators of mites can often need protection from the vagaries of the winter weather, in order to survive in sufficient numbers to start controlling the emerging pest mites in spring.

A further point to note is that fungicides can also seriously damage the population of mite predators, especially predatory mites, which appear to succumb quite easily to fungicides. Winter washes are not organic and can be most damaging to predators and great care and consideration should be given to the problem before applying such treatments.

Unlike aphid populations, which can increase very dramatically, spider mite populations build up steadily, but can just as steadily be reduced by predators. Unfortunately, this can be a problem, as the voracious appetite of some predators can actually reduce their future success as they consume their 'larder' often to a level that can no longer sustain them, resulting in their need to move on. In this way it is possible for the spider mite population to recover without the balance of predators to control them.

Bryobia mites, long confused as being red spider mites, require similar treatment to control them naturally, with not only adequate stocks of predators, but also over-wintering accommodation. Similar to other mites, bryobia may be predated upon by such creatures as anthocorid bugs, black-kneed capsids, the small black ladybird, *Stethorus punctillum* and another type of mite called typhlodromid mite. One particular capsid, *Coniortodes salicellus,* the capsid bug

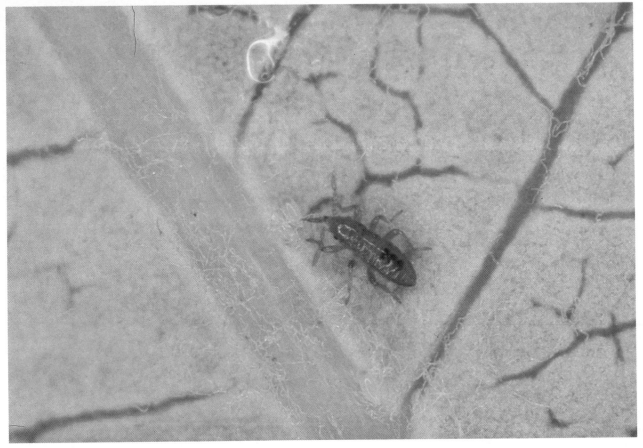

appears to readily predate upon the various life stages of the bryobia and may therefore be especially beneficial.

Sadly though, it has to be stated that in most cases these predators may just about hold their own and often fail to hold the rapid build-up of the infestation. This can be made all the more difficult by thoughtless applications of insecticides or fungicides, even organic materials, to control other pests. The effect of this is that it can seriously disturb the balance and often eliminate the beneficial predators, whilst hardly touching the mite pests.

Scale insects

Scale insects can often be one of the most difficult pests to control due to the waxy scale which acts as a shield to protect the insect within. Varying in shape and form, scale insects may be sometimes termed brown scales, mussel scales, oystershell scales, pear scales and woolly scales.

Fortunately, there are several natural biological controls for them, although some are not really feasible when plants are grown under glass, when infestations of scale insects can be a very real problem.

The blister-like insects remain relatively static for most of their lives, except when they first hatch and lumber off to find a position to feed. During this period, even though the cuticle of the scale thickens, the pest may be parasitised especially by parasitic wasps. The tiny *Aphytis mytilaspidis* or chalcid wasp is a very effective parasite on mussel scales and oystershell scales into which are laid the eggs of the parasite, which on hatching consume the scale insect.

Wild birds, most often tits, can predate upon the mature woolly scales. Woolly scales may also be attacked by some types of fly larvae of *Leucopis spp.* which again predate upon the pest.

Other types of wasp such as *Coccophagus lycimnia* are particularly active as parasites upon the brown scale insect, whilst the pear scale is not only attacked by parasitic wasps, but may also fall victim to the very valuable, almost invaluable anthocorid bug, which is an insect with a voracious appetite for plant pests. Pear scales may also be predated upon by mites, as well as adult and larval stages of a ladybird beetle *Chilocorus renipustulatus.*

Slugs and snails

A well planned garden, complete with a garden pond, sufficient cover and possibly areas that are kept a little less tidy, should help to encourage hedgehogs and frogs to the garden. These

very valuable creatures are very useful in helping to control slugs, which can be so damaging in their ravaging effects upon plant life.

Hedgehogs can be encouraged by the provision of hibernation and nesting facilities. Frogs can be encouraged by a small pond with nearby cover in the form of long grass. If tadpoles can be obtained from an obliging friend or neighbour's pond and are placed in the pond, it should be possible to encourage a self-regenerating population of these real friends to the gardener within a few years.

Above:
Hedgehogs help control slugs and snails.

Left:
Snails are one of the most destructive pests in the garden.

Above:
Another useful predator of slugs and snails.

The larvae can be very difficult to control using organic treatments, as the insect produces an increasingly thicker cuticle or cover for its body, as it progresses through its various larval stages. The larvae, or scales, are small oval scale-like objects that are creamy white in colour.

Fortunately for the gardener, there is an extremely efficient commercially available parasite which must be one of the most ideal parasites. The parasite, in the form of a small parasitic wasp called *Encarsia formosa,* lays its eggs in the larval scale stages of the whitefly's life cycle. Once parasitised effectively the scales then clearly turn black, enabling one to easily identify just how effective the level of control is. Hopefully, as the encarsia wasp increases in population, the number of black scales will increase signalling the decline of the whitefly infestation.

Encarsia formosa can be purchased as pupae on cardboard strips, which can be easily sent through the post. These strips are simply placed amongst the crop that is infested with whitefly until such time as the pupae hatch into adult wasps. Once these have mated the females search for the larval scales of the whitefly to parasitise by laying their eggs within the bodies of the larvae.

Similar to the red spider mite predator, *Phytoseiulus persimilis,* the encarsia wasp prefers warm temperatures to be most active. Ideally, a minimum temperature of 15°C (60°F) and an average temperature of 18-24°C (65-75°F) should be maintained in the glasshouse or conservatory.

Sadly, because of its need for relatively warm conditions, the encarsia wasp is only really effective under glass during the spring to autumn period and is most unlikely to be effective, or even survive during the winter period.

Centipedes can also be useful in helping to control slugs, and similar to hedgehogs and frogs may also help to keep down other insect pests as well.

Apple and pear suckers

One could be forgiven for mistaking or confusing the identification of a young apple or pear sucker with that of an aphid, until closer inspection shows the obvious differences.

The pest can be a real nuisance to fruit trees and like so many insect pests it normally over-winters well. From the egg, which is the over-wintering stage, the insect hatches and devastates the fruit tree blossom.

Fortunately, the pest is yet another menu item of our favourite all-round predator, the anthocorid bug, which consumes not only the young apple and pear suckers, but also the eggs as well.

Whitefly

Whitefly are tiny moth-like insects which can be a real menace especially under glass where the adults fly up at the least disturbance and can then be a real aggravation and irritation. Although the adult may annoy the gardener, it is the larvae that feed on the plant that cause the plant damage.

Source of supply

Most organic products are readily available from Garden Centres, DIY Centres, Hardware and Garden Shops and even some Chemists.

However, a very comprehensive range of products is available from Chase Organics who also supply a number of predators and parasites.

As far as most naturally occurring predators and parasites are concerned, it is sensible to leave parts of the garden 'wild' to encourage a more natural balance and to provide ideal conditions. Careful thought to protect such areas and to provide nesting, breeding, feeding and over-wintering areas will pay dividends.

6
Pests and Diseases

Ants

Ants are not usually regarded as a plant pest, for they cause relatively minor damage to leaf tissue by removing the odd piece of leaf or so, with little overall effect upon the plant. However, due to their subterranean nesting activities, they can cause greater damage to plants by their industrious burrowing. Small heaps or mounds of fine powdery soil betray the ant colony. So intensive is their tunnelling that they can indirectly cause damage to plants by literally undermining the plant's roots. At best this may just cause a minor check to the plant or plants, but at worst the root system may be so damaged by the collapse of the soil structure that the plant may fall over or wilt and die.

One could perhaps forgive this activity if this was in isolation; however, ants have a rather bad name because of their association with one of the gardener's most common pests, the aphid. Ants actually farm aphids and make use of the honeydew that aphids excrete in much the same way that dairy cows are farmed by man for their milk. As part of this farming activity, ants not only tend their 'herd' of aphids, but also physically move aphids around and help to protect them against some of their natural enemies. This association can therefore tend to render the ant as an indirect pest to be controlled along with its other nuisance role as a household pest.

Ants are attracted by spillages of sugar and other sweet products, where crumbs may fall and act as a magnet to the insect as it forages for food. However, in weighing up whether or not the insect should be controlled, one should first reflect on the fact that ants can be beneficial by attacking other insects that are pests. Where possible it is perhaps better to try to deter them from certain areas, rather than killing them.

Ants are social insects and live in a colony working for the common good in much the same way as bees, with a queen at the centre producing eggs which hatch into larvae for the workers to feed. Favourite nesting sites are under brick pavers or concrete flagstones, as well as under, or close to paths or walls.

● **Control:** Where ants are a pest because of their association with aphids, plan ahead and where possible use grease-bands on plants such as fruit trees, to prevent ants crossing over them to 'farm' aphids.

Alternatively, aphids can be deterred by planting *Tagetes patula* (French or African Marigold) where you do not wish to see ants. This can be close to plants where aphid 'farming' could be a problem or close to seedlings or seed trays, where undermining could reduce vigour or success. Planting close to the house may help to prevent their entry into the home, particularly if planted near to air-bricks or cracks in the wall where ants could gain easy access to the house.

Once you have found the nest it can be seriously damaged, if not destroyed, by being soaked with boiling water. This has the advantage of being very localised in its effect. Take care though when conveying the boiling water not to be scalded and to hold the kettle carefully, with the spout pointing away from yourself.

Ants can also be killed using pyrethrum and derris, although the effect is one of only reducing the colony's activity for a short time. A more ingenious, if perhaps somewhat ghastly technique is to poison the colony by persuading the worker ants to carry back poison to the nest. However, this technique is not organically acceptable as it relies on borax mixed with sugar in solution and placed on a small flat piece of glass or plastic close to where ants forage. This will soon attract them in numbers and when collected and taken back to the colony, often results in the poisoning and death of the colony.

Proprietary solutions of borax are readily available and should be used rather than making your own, due to the level of toxicity of the material. Do not be tempted to formulate your own pesticide brews as the Food and Environment Protection Act (1987) forbids the manufacture and formulation of 'home remedies' and requires the use of approved products. Besides, home-made solutions are always dubious in quality and their level of safety. Take care also to place the poison well away from where children, pets or livestock could be accidentally exposed to it and remove the piece of glass or plastic as soon as the task is completed.

Aphids

Aphids, the somewhat elongated, globular and fleshy insect pests, are probably the most common and most damaging pests that affect a wide range of plants and crops. Most often referred to as 'greenfly', the aphid family is very large with many relatives that are equally damaging. These include the black bean aphid, cabbage aphid, currant blister aphid, mealy plum aphid, peach potato aphid, plum aphid, root aphid, rosy apple aphid and woolly aphid, to name but a few of the more common ones.

With the exception of root aphids, which are a pest of the root zone, aphids are a particular problem of soft growing tips, flower buds and young plant tissue. Aphids have a long protrusion called a stylet, which is stabbed into the plant's tissue and through which the sap is absorbed.

The damage caused can be very severe in a short space of time due to the young growth being attacked. The rate of reproduction of the aphid is also extremely fast and as the adult aphids give birth to offspring that feed immediately on being born, they need to be controlled without delay.

Apart from the damage caused through the season, aphids can become a pest problem very early in the next season, as the over-wintered egg produced at the end of the previous season hatches and the newly emerged aphid reproduces without delay.

Not only do aphids cause severe deformation of the growth of the affected plant, but they can also be carriers of disease. Aphids are known vectors of plant virus diseases which cannot be cured on affected plants such as strawberries. The honeydew excreted by aphids also attracts sooty mould to grow on the sticky excrement, which can be a particular nuisance on plants cultivated for their decorative effect.

Right:
Aphids, aided by ants, attacking soft fruit.

● **Control:** Aphids are relatively easy to control, provided that they are treated as soon as the infestation is identified. Repeated treatments at 7 to 10-day intervals may be necessary to effect complete control.

Relying only on natural control methods such as hover-flies, ladybirds, anthocorid bugs, birds and fungi is rarely successful when growing cultivated plants and most often one needs to resort to using pesticides to eradicate the pest.

Pyrethrum and derris are particularly good at controlling aphids. Pyrethrum is probably the most popular insecticide

used as a spray, although soft soap is also a useful material. High-pressure water jets may sometimes help to reduce an aphid population, but is rarely that effective, particularly on larger plants.

Root aphids are not easy to control and infested plants may have to be destroyed, if the treatment is not satisfactory, as organic pesticides are unfortunately not that effective as a drench.

Bacterial diseases

Bacterial problems are particularly difficult, in that although relatively infrequent, they are extremely difficult to control. Certain leaf spots can be caused by bacteria, which are hard to distinguish from fungal spots. Sometimes bacterial 'ooze' may be seen or a 'watersoaked' edge to the spot may be evident. However, these can in no way be seen as a definitive diagnosis and analysis may need to be carried out by a plant pathologist when circumstances dictate the necessity.

Other forms of bacterial problem cause fireblight which is a notifiable disease of rosaceous plants including hawthorn, roses, cotoneaster, pyracantha, apples and pears. Bacterial canker is a further problem caused by bacteria.

The disease can be most often spread by physical contact, wind and water, which washes or splashes the bacteria from infected to uninfected plants.

● **Control:** Bacterial problems are almost impossible to control and are best prevented, using copper as a spray to help prevent infection. Any diseased leaves or parts of plants should be hygienically removed and burned, taking care to notify the Ministry of Agriculture, Fisheries and Food if the notifiable disease fireblight is discovered.

Beetles

Before condemning all beetles as pests, it is important to note that many beetles are very useful creatures and help to keep down many insect pests. Probably the best known beneficial beetle is the ladybird and its fiercesome-looking larvae that predate greedily on aphids.

However, there are many other beetles that can be a real problem. Amongst these is the asparagus beetle which has yellow and black wing cases on the adult and greyish-black larvae, both of which feed on asparagus plants, severely damaging stems and leaves.

Flea beetles not only cause damage to many plants including brassicas in particular, by eating holes in the leaves, but can also

Left:
Raspberry beetle larva on fruit. Sadly by the time it is discovered, the damage has already started on the crop.
Crown Copyright

62

Above, above right and right:
Many beetles are useful creatures and help to keep down insect pests. The best known beneficial beetle is the ladybird which is a voracious predator of aphids.

Facing page, left:
Perhaps the occasional worm can be allowed especially as the thrush is very useful at controlling snails. *RSPB*

Facing page, right:
The great tit and other members of the tit family have a voracious appetite for caterpillars and aphids, especially when this valuable source of protein is in demand when the young are being raised. *RSPB*

convey and transmit some virus diseases. So called because the beetles jump somewhat similar to fleas, the adult flea beetles are also known insect pests of ornamental plants including alyssum, anemone, nasturtium and members of the cruciferae family.

Although asparagus and flea beetles are particularly active in the spring, other beetles are especially problematic later in the season. Such is the case with the raspberry beetle, which is also

a pest of blackberries and loganberries and is also probably one of the best known pest beetles. Hours spent blackberrying in the woods are perhaps most remembered from cautiously biting each berry first to inspect the inside for the possibility of the presence of a grub which is the larva of the raspberry beetle.

Strawberry beetles are quite different to raspberry beetles and consume the exterior of the fruit, taking cover at the base of the plant amongst straw or other litter, including dead leaves.

● **Control:** Beetles can be difficult to control, particularly if the damage is caused by beetle larvae within the plant or its fruit. To effect control, it is essential to spray early enough before the insect enters the plant.

Spraying with derris in the spring will help control asparagus and flea beetles and later in the summer when flowers are visible to help control raspberry and strawberry beetles. Repeated applications may be found necessary to ensure that the pests are adequately treated. Alternatively the use of polypropylene fabric (Agryll) will help to act as a useful physical barrier.

As beetles can over-winter quite easily in the garden, take care to ensure that any dead foliage or litter is removed, especially from areas where cultivated plants or crops are to be grown. Wherever possible, prevention is better than cure, otherwise spray or dust treatments will need to be resorted to, to control the pest prior to egg laying. Treating late will result in the larvae causing damage which cannot be remedied.

Far left:
Wherever possible, natural or artificial nesting sites should be provided to encourage wild birds. By helping to increase the bird population year round, many pests will be kept under control. *RSPB*

Centre left:
Robins really are the gardener's friend and help to control a wide range of garden insect pests. Apart from providing nesting sites, occasionally turn over a small area of garden soil to expose insects and worms and encourage the robin. *RSPB*

Left:
Unusual nesting sites are often chosen by wild birds in and around the garden. Apart from nesting boxes, even kettles and flower pots may be occupied. *RSPB*

Birds

Similar to beetles, not all birds cause damage in the garden and there are many that are extremely beneficial. Thrushes are particularly good at keeping snails down, whereas at the other end of the size spectrum, blue tits, great tits and other members of the titmouse family are particularly active feeders on aphids and caterpillars. However, such birds as pigeons, bullfinches and sparrows can be particularly damaging and a real nuisance.

Pigeons can wreak havoc amongst cultivated food crops and sparrows appear to carry out mischievous antics by pulling up seedlings and even onion sets, almost for the fun of it. Sadly, the beautifully coloured bullfinch can severely damage flower buds on fruit trees early in the spring and even blackbirds can be a nuisance for the damage caused to soft fruit, especially to redcurrants, blackcurrants and strawberries.

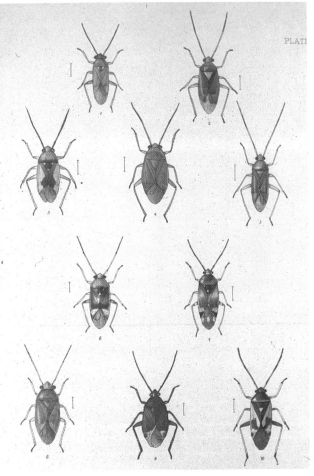

Above:
Bullfinches can be a nuisance to the fruit grower for the damage that they cause to blossom. At such a time it is worth covering bushes or trees with a protective net. *RSPB*

Above right:
The capsid family parasitise plants as well as predating upon other insects. Sadly, they often appear to cause more damage to plants than they are noted for beneficial effects upon pests.
Crown Copyright

● **Control:** Control of birds as a pest or nuisance should not be considered for many reasons ranging from environmental to matters of legislation and even practicality. It is better to consider preventative measures to minimise damage. Cats are obvious deterrents, but they themselves can cause damage in the garden by scratching up seed-beds and areas where young plants have just been planted.

Humming line and foil strips may be found to be useful if often only for a limited period, when used at an appropriate time such as early spring, to minimise damage by helping to frighten off birds.

Where possible, the best method is to use fine netting to cover seedbeds, fruit bushes and trees to prevent entry by birds that could cause damage to flower buds and fruit. However, take care to inspect netting regularly to free any trapped birds, to avoid causing any unfortunate and unnecessary distress, suffering or death. Try where possible to use proprietary bird webbing or netting that is designed to allow birds to escape without injury, whilst still acting as an efficient deterrent.

Capsid bugs

Capsid bugs are another pest that can cause severe damage to cultivated plants because of their feeding activity on young leaf tissue. Feeding in a similar manner to aphids and in some respects bearing a close resemblance, with colours ranging from light yellow to reddish-brown, with others that are of a green hue.

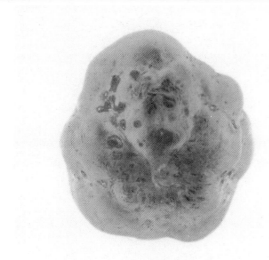

examined for pest damage. Apart from damaging young growth, capsids also harm fruit as it grows. Both the adults and the young larvae (called nymphs) cause ill-effects on a wide range of plants including top fruit and soft fruit, as well as many ornamental plants such as asters, chrysanthemums, dahlias, nasturtiums, roses, salvias and zinnias.

● **Control:** Capsids can be controlled with sprays of pyrethrum or derris applied in early spring and with successive treatments as necessary. Soft fruit should be sprayed just before flowering and repeated after 10-14 days. Top fruit should be treated just after flowering with successive treatments at appropriate intervals to effect control of the pest before damage occurs. Ornamental crops should be treated as necessary with an interval varying between seven and 14 days to gain control.

Capsids can over-winter in leaf litter and other plant debris and their numbers may be reduced the following season by attempting to tidy up in the autumn to remove or reduce the cover available to the pest.

Caterpillars

The range of caterpillars that are responsible for plant damage is very large indeed, as is the type of damage caused. Caterpillars are the larvae of butterflies or moths that generally

Left:
Typical damage to fruit caused by capsids. Once damaged the area affected becomes worse and very unsightly.
Crown Copyright

Below:
Cabbage white caterpillars have a voracious appetite, particularly for brassica leaves. The dramatic rate of damage is remarkable and requires early treatment. *Crown Copyright*

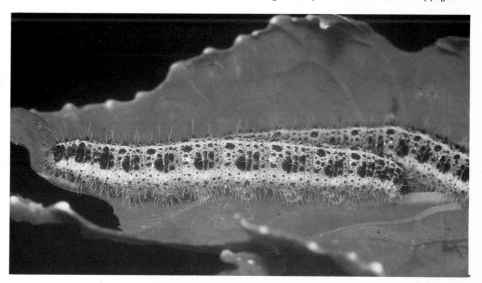

Although some species predate on other plant pests, most of the capsids that are commonly seen are apple capsids, common green capsids and potato capsids, which cause severe damage to plants by perforating the young tissue and feeding on the sap. Severe deformation of the plant's growth results in much the same way as with aphid infestations.

Unlike aphids, which are much slower moving, capsids are quite active and will quickly fly off when the foliage is being

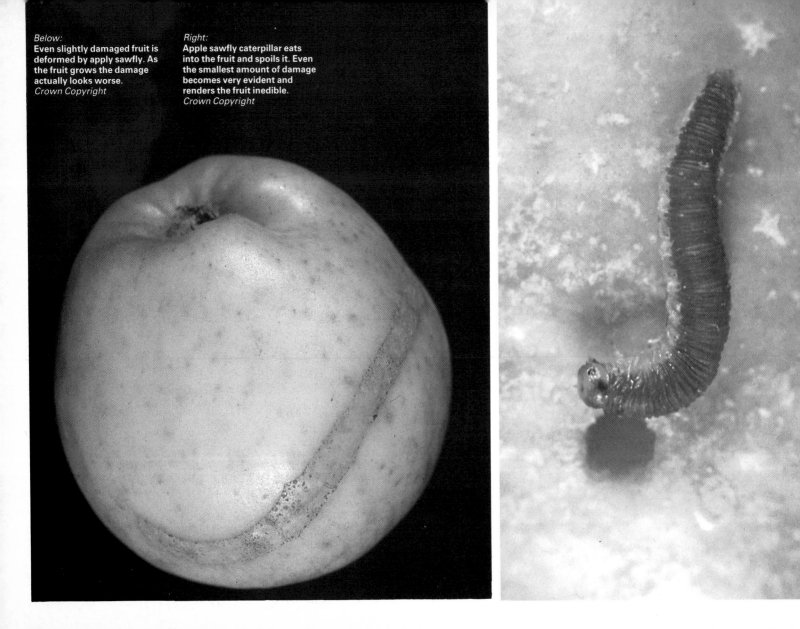

Below:
Even slightly damaged fruit is deformed by apply sawfly. As the fruit grows the damage actually looks worse.
Crown Copyright

Right:
Apple sawfly caterpillar eats into the fruit and spoils it. Even the smallest amount of damage becomes very evident and renders the fruit inedible.
Crown Copyright

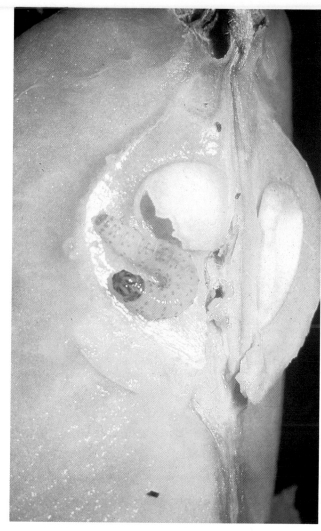

Apple sawfly caterpillars eat into fruit such as apples and pears, causing spoiling of the fruit, which then falls from the tree prior to their normal harvest, whilst those less severely damaged show scar damage and produce misshapen fruits. Over-wintering as larvae in cocoons in the garden soil, the adults emerge the following spring. They mate and lay their eggs into the fruit blossom. The larvae then hatch and burrow into the growing fruit. Similar species such as common gooseberry sawfly and plum sawfly can also be problematic along with many other sawfly species including leaf-rolling sawfly.

Cabbage white caterpillars can be very damaging to brassicas and soon after the eggs have been laid on the lower surface of leaves, the caterpillars emerge and consume vast quantities of leaf tissue, often right back to the veins. The caterpillars also tunnel into the centre of the plant causing massive damage and spoiling of the plant. Cabbage white butterflies over-winter as pupae, from which emerge adults the following spring.

Codling moth larvae cause similar damage to sawfly, burrowing into the young fruit of apples and pears, the eggs being laid on the surface of the fruit. Larvae generally pupate wherever they can find cover on or around the tree, emerging

Above:
Codling moth larvae burrow into the young fruit of apples and pears. Early treatment and control is therefore absolutely essential. *Crown Copyright*

Left:
Typical signs of attack by codling moth larvae. It is now too late for treatment and the problems will only get worse. *Crown Copyright*

have a voracious appetite, consuming large volumes of plant tissue. Many caterpillars cause most damage to leaves, stripping the foliage to the veins, whilst others burrow into stems or consume growing tips.

from their cocoons the following spring, unless the weather is conducive to an early pupation and emergence in September of the same year.

Pea moths can be quite a problem after the eggs have been laid on the plants. The emerging caterpillars burrow into the pods and eat the young peas inside. The caterpillars then pupate in the garden soil in a cocoon, to emerge the following spring.

Tortrix moths must be one of the most damaging caterpillar pests, particularly of ornamental plants such as euonymus and peperomia. For some time the damage is not immediately evident as the caterpillar spins the young leaves together to protect itself, whilst it feeds within on the young foliage, before pupating.

Cutworm caterpillars emerge from the soil and eat the base of plant stems of many ornamentals including asters, chrysanthemums, dahlias and zinnias, causing wilting or total collapse of the plant. The larvae pupate in the soil and over-winter to emerge as moths the following spring.

● **Control:** Caterpillars can be effectively controlled by spraying with derris or pyrethrum. Spraying with the biological control bacterial agent *Bacillus thuringiensis* can be particularly effective where the tissue sprayed is likely to be consumed by the insect. Crucial timing of spraying is essential, otherwise late applications of sprays are useless, particularly for pests such as sawfly where the pest is inside the plant.

Good garden hygiene is also worthwhile to remove cover in the form of leaf litter and autumn cultivation to expose any pupae in the soil.

Grease-bands may also have some effect in reducing movement, as may pheremone traps to catch male insects to prevent mating. Dusting around the base of plants with derris may help to control such caterpillars as cutworm.

Cats

Cats can be more than a nuisance in the garden, although their presence in helping to chase birds away and to help keep mice and rats at bay should be considered in their defence.

Cats can be particularly annoying in their toilet activities particularly amongst newly planted plants or seedbeds, where their energetic scratching can ruin a day's gardening in a few moments.

Apart from damaging and fouling newly planted areas, cats can also cause great damage to young trees by their frantic claw sharpening. Bark can be torn off to expose the tree to infections and possible consequent loss.

Facing page, top:
Emerging caterpillars of the pea moth eat the young peas in the pod, resulting in damage that is not seen until later.
Crown Copyright

Facing page, bottom:
Tortrix moth caterpillars spin silk to tie leaves together. When this occurs with the growing tips, severe damage and deformation can occur.
Crown Copyright

Left:
Cutworm caterpillars eat the base of plant stems, with the obvious severe effects upon the plants. *Crown Copyright*

● **Control:** Clearly cats cannot be controlled, but their nuisance effects can be minimised by various techniques. The use of physical barriers in the form of hedging such as hawthorn can help to reduce their entry into the garden. Spraying with repellents containing citrus oil or oil of citronella can also be effective, if only for a short period. Orange peel can be useful when small pieces measuring approximately 2-3cm (1in) square are scattered over and around seed beds, where the pungent aroma helps to deter cats effectively.

Newly planted trees can be protected from being used as scratching posts by covering with a perforated plastic tree guard or by wrapping chicken wire loosely around the trunk. In either case take care to ensure that the guard covers at least 75cm (2ft 6in) of the trunk. This can also help to protect against damage caused by rabbits and deer if the height of the guard is raised.

In the short term pepper dust can be fairly effective, but strong winds and rain nullify its effect.

Alternatively, one could always keep a dog, but they too can be a problem in their own right!

Dogs

Dogs are another pest, which similar to cats are more of a pest or real nuisance when they belong to somebody else.

Dogs can also ruin newly planted areas or seed beds by their ridiculous scratching and digging, which seems to achieve little except for possibly spreading the results of the activity to the four winds.

Below:
Earwigs can be a real nuisance. They seem to like some flowers — like the Zinnia seen here — better than others!
Chase Organics Ltd

A further problem with dogs results from their urinating on lawns or up trees or bushes. Whilst scorched areas of lawn can in time recover and regrow, bushes and foliage of plants, especially conifers, can be seriously damaged. In the case of conifers the damage may take several years to grow over resulting in a real eyesore for some considerable time.

● **Control:** Prevention has to be better than cure and sadly the only effective way to prevent problems with dogs is by excluding them from the garden. To some degree dogs are easier to keep out of a garden than cats and apart from fencing, a thorny hedge may be found to be effective.

Trees or shrubs planted in exposed positions are perhaps best protected by a chicken wire barrier to prevent dogs getting too close to urinate on them.

Earwigs

Earwigs can be a real nuisance on a number of ornamental plants, most commonly dahlias and chrysanthemums, but also cinerarias, delphiniums, pansies, violas and zinnias.

This insect is most active at night when it does its damage by feeding on leaves, flowers and buds. The damage takes the form of irregular cuts and holes in flower petals and leaves. During the day these long, ugly insects, with fiercesome-looking pincers at their rear ends, hide amongst the foliage or in nearby litter or rubbish. In late summer they can often be found on apples and other top fruit, especially where there are holes present for them to hide in.

Apart from eating plant material, earwigs also have some beneficial activity in the garden by preying upon some other insect pests including aphids.

Over-wintering sites for the earwig adult is usually compost leaf litter and under paving stones, loose brickwork and decaying or splitting wood.

● **Control:** Derris is reasonably effective at controlling earwigs when used as a spray or dust, although the dust can tend to leave an unsightly deposit.

A further technique worth trying is to trap them using small flowerpots or yoghurt pots filled with straw, hay or wood wool, which are inverted and placed on canes amongst the infected plants. These should be put in place during the day and removed the following morning after being left overnight. The pots should then have their contents removed, exposing the earwigs that have sought refuge. The offending insects can then be dispatched or perhaps more humanely removed to the compost heap where they can do little harm.

Eelworm

Eelworm are from the nematode family, of which there are many beneficial as well as damaging types. Nematodes are very active in breaking down organic matter and fulfil a vital function in the healthy balance of micro-organisms in garden soil and compost.

However, as a pest eelworms are extremely destructive for their microscopic size and severely check and mutate the growth of plants. Eelworm can be found either in the leaves and growing shoots and buds within the plant's stem or in the roots, where their activities result in irregular-shaped cysts on the roots.

Bulbs are often infected with eelworm even when purchased as new stock and other ornamentals such as hydrangea and chrysanthemum may also be infected even when acquired as new plants. Crops such as strawberry can be infected with leaf eelworm, whilst potatoes and tomatoes can be infected with cyst and root knot eelworm.

Apart from causing obvious deformation of the growth, eelworm can result in premature death of plants at worst and at least in much reduced cropping potential. The worm-like eelworm can only be seen under a microscope and it is their damaging effects that are most often seen.

● **Control:** There is no organic method of controlling eelworm apart from using hot water treatment for plants such as strawberries, bulbs and chrysanthemum stools when the dormant bulbs or stools are immersed in water at 46°C (115°F) for 5min prior to being plunged into cold water afterwards to minimise damage. Some bulbs such as narcissus may be treated at a lower temperature of 44°C (112°F) for up to 3hr followed by controlled cooling.

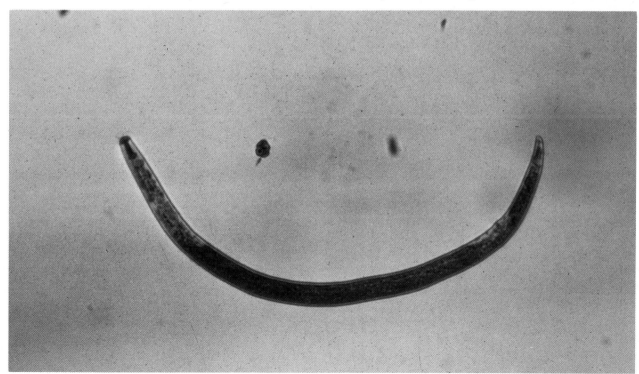

Left:
The worm-like eelworm is very tiny and can only be seen under a microscope. Nevertheless, the damage caused can be severe, resulting in deformation of growth and much reduced potential. *Crown Copyright*

Although hot-water treatment is reasonably effective, it can cause damage to the plant and great care should be exercised and should perhaps only be used as the last resort prior to the only really effective method of rogueing out infected plants and destroying them, preferably on the bonfire.

Crop rotation to reduce root eelworm on potatoes and tomatoes may help to minimise the problem, along with the use of French or African Marigolds which when planted nearby, help to keep eelworm away. Also look for eelworm-resistant varieties of potatoes such as Maris Piper to help keep the problem to a minimum.

Flies

When the word fly is used, one immediately thinks of the common housefly. However, from the family come useful types such as the hover-fly which predates upon aphids as well as plant pests such as leaf miners, leatherjackets and root flies.

Cabbage root flies cause severe damage to many members of the brassica family apart from just cabbages, including cauliflowers, Brussels sprouts, radishes and even wallflowers which are all from the same family.

However, over-wintered as pupae in the soil, the emerging adults come out and lay their eggs close to or on the stems of newly transplanted plants. The eggs then hatch and the larvae cause considerable damage to the stems resulting in either a severe check to growth and cropping potential, or at worst the early death of the plant. The larvae then pupate and may be followed by another one or two generations.

Carrot fly act in much the same way by eggs being laid close to the carrots hatching into larvae, which tunnel into and around the fleshy root. This results in damage to the actual root and premature leaf wilting and loss, although it is by far the actual damage to the carrot itself which can render them useless. Larvae pupate in the nearby soil and are usually followed by a second generation.

It is the larvae again that is the problem with leaf miners that infest chrysanthemum, celery, beetroot, cineraria and even the tough-leaved holly. The adult lays eggs into the leaf which hatch into larvae which tunnel or 'mine' between the upper and lower leaf surfaces.

Leatherjackets are the damaging larvae of crane-flies or daddy-longlegs which are often seen in large numbers in the early autumn in September following the larvae's pupation. Leatherjackets damage young plants, where they feed on the roots of brassicas, strawberries, lettuce and even grass. Damage to young plants is most likely to manifest itself as sudden wilt and losses, with minor infestations resulting in a severe check to growth. Lawns infested with leatherjackets will show up the damage as yellowish patches.

Onion fly attack onions by the damaging effects of the larvae on the bulbs and stems of plants including leeks and shallots. The larvae pupate in the soil and hatch to produce adults that mate and lay eggs on the plant or in the soil close by. Anything up to four generations of onion fly may be produced in a year.

● **Control:** Depending on the type of fly, control needs to be tailored to the specific pest. Pyrethrum or derris may be reasonably effective at controlling adult flies, but for many pests this is usually found to be impractical.

Leaf miners can really only be killed by systemic insecticides and so the organic gardener may have to resort to squashing the larvae within the leaf, or removing and burning the infested leaves.

Barrier methods may also be found to be useful for controlling such pests and cabbage root fly. Polypropylene fabric may also be effective for controlling cabbage root fly and carrot fly by

Centre:
Cabbage root fly larvae on a turnip. Once the fly has laid its eggs near the base of the plant the larvae hatch and burrow into the plant. *Crown Copyright*

Left:
Onion fly larvae damage the stems, roots and bulbs in much the same way as cabbage root fly. *Crown Copyright*

Right:
Leatherjackets damage the roots of a wide range of plants including grass and can be very difficult to control.
Crown Copyright

Centre right:
Rust diseases affect a wide range of plants. The fungus takes nutrition from the host plant and can deform and spoil the plant's appearance as well as reducing yield.
Crown Copyright

Far right:
Downy mildew on the seed leaves of brassicas. Early action must be taken to prevent or control the organism.
Crown Copyright

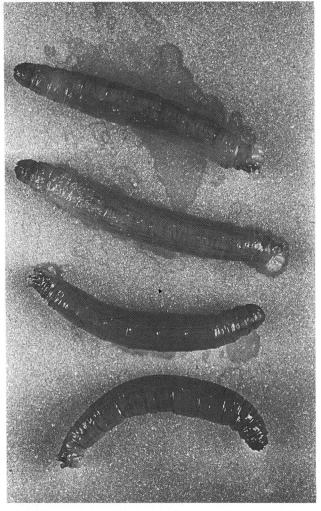

preventing their access to the plants. Brassica collars, consisting of an impervious membrane placed around the stem, help to prevent the adult fly laying eggs close to the plant.

Chamomile may also help to deter onion fly when planted nearby.

As far as leatherjackets are concerned, cultural treatment during the winter, by thorough digging, may expose the pupae which can be destroyed. On lawns a somewhat tedious yet moderately effective technique is to drench the lawn very thoroughly and cover overnight with a heavy waterproof sheet or black polythene that is weighted down well. The following morning when the sheeting is removed, the larvae which have been encouraged to the surface can then be exposed and dispatched.

Froghoppers

Froghoppers must surely be one of the best remembered insects from one's childhood. Children have long been fascinated by the frothy cuckoo spit seen on the stems of a wide range of plants including asters, chrysanthemums, roses, blackberries and raspberries. This is produced by the young nymphs which produce the mass of bubbles from their rear end, to protect themselves from drying-out.

The common froghopper causes relatively minor damage and may be found feeding upon the sap of plants as a pale green nymph which can be exposed under the bubbles by teasing away the froth or simply blowing it away to expose the small insect.

The red and black froghopper is somewhat larger than the common froghopper and feeds on top fruit such as apples and pears, as well as soft fruit such as strawberries, blackberries and raspberries.

Most feeding activity is on plant leaves and stems, although roots may also be attacked. However, the damage is most unlikely to be severe and rarely warrants treatment unless the volume of cuckoo spit in evidence becomes a nuisance and damage such as leaf deformation is seen.

The insects, not unlike a frog in shape but of a tiny size, have very strong rear legs. As adults they hop off when exposed, unlike the nymph which tries to remain hidden in the mass of bubbles. At the end of the season the adults die, having laid eggs to over-winter until the next year, when the insect may start to become a problem in April or May.

● **Control:** Froghoppers are really of little consequence and may be controlled quite easily by physical or chemical means. When only a few patches of bubbles are seen, the cuckoo spit can be removed with a small paint brush or strong jet of water to wash away the nymphs and adults.

Alternatively, froghoppers may be controlled with derris or pyrethrum, if ever the infestation becomes severe.

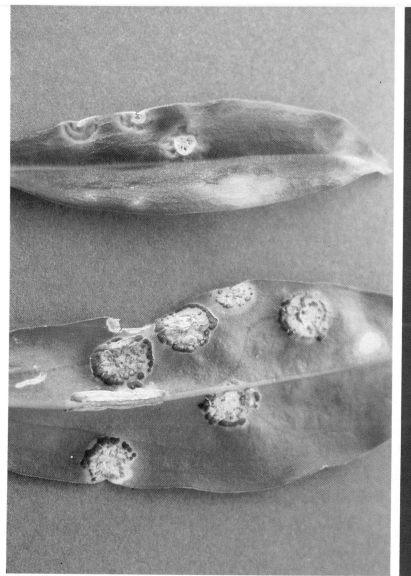
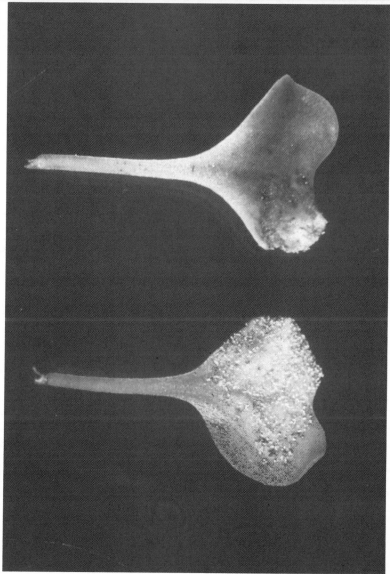

Fungal diseases

The primitive range of plants called fungi do not possess the green pigment chlorophyll to manufacture food for themselves and so they need to obtain nutrients from a readily available source. Some fungi are beneficial fungi that are saprophytic and live on dead and decaying organic matter, eg mushrooms. Others are parasitic and live on living tissue which is normally that of higher plants, but may also be that of animals or insects, eg mildew and athlete's foot.

There is an enormous range of fungi that affect plants, some only marginally, at worst spoiling the appearance and reducing the yield and cropping potential, whilst others attack and destroy the plants.

Fungi that parasitise upon a plant and yet rely on the plant to continue to live are sometimes called obligative fungi and include such as mildews, rusts and leaf-spotting fungi. Whereas fungi that attack a living plant and can then continue to live on the decaying matter are sometimes called facultative, examples of which are honey fungus and damping-off disease.

Leaf spots affect a wide range of plants and cause mostly regular-shaped spots on foliage, although many may manifest themselves as a spot that covers a large part of the leaf including its edge.

Rust diseases take on a different form in that as the fungus produces spores, the spore-bearing bodies may be seen to be raised quite proud from the foliage surface, with coloured spots of red, yellow, brown and other hues. Rust diseases are more likely to be specific to particular plants than some other fungal diseases such as antirrhinum rust and carnation rust.

Mildew is often seen as the two common forms of downy mildew and powdery mildew. Downy mildew appears to prefer more damp conditions that favour the growth and spread of the fungus with spots producing a raised profile of spore-bearing bodies, whereas powdery mildews seem to prefer a drier environment, the fungus and its spores covering often quite large areas of the leaf surface.

Scab diseases infect apples and pears and produce brown spots that crack and allow other fungi to enter through the wound and damage the fruit still further.

Damping-off diseases cause stem or root rots and diseases such as grey mould quite often occur when cultural conditions are not quite right for the plant, but instead favour the growth of the fungus. A typical example of this is the damping-off of seedlings, which usually occurs when seedlings are grown too closely together and tend to weaken, producing elongated stems which are susceptible to attack by fungi if kept too moist. Poor hygiene can also accentuate the problem, as can be the case with cyclamen or strawberries, which on contracting grey-mould disease on dead and decaying leaves or fruits may suffer far more seriously if the infected parts of the plant are not cleanly and swiftly removed.

Many fungal problems can be reduced by improved garden hygiene and good cultivation practice. Simply clearing up fallen leaf litter and dead plant material in the autumn, especially from around plants known to suffer from fungal diseases, can help to reduce the problems encountered the following year. Many fungal spores are produced throughout the growing season and prior to the autumn, those that will over-winter on leaf litter and other plant material would, if not cleared up, proffer a considerable threat to re-infect the following year.

● **Control:** For the organic gardener the range of control measures to minimise the effects of fungal problems is more than somewhat limited. Greater emphasis therefore has to be placed on improved cultural techniques and hygiene measures, backed-up by the very few fungicides that can be considered for organic use. Sadly, those available provide no systemic activity

Below:
Powdery mildew on the leaf of an acer. The disease can be a real problem on ornamental as well as food crops.
Crown Copyright

to prevent and help control fungi, or materials to drench plants to control root and stem diseases.

Basically, the range is limited to materials formulated from copper or sulphur. Sulphur brings its own problems in that many varieties of top fruit and soft fruit are known to be sulphur-shy, in other words can be damaged by the material.

Copper, formulated as Bordeaux mixture, may help to control blight, downy mildew, apple scab (when applied at pink bud stage) various leaf spots and rusts, provided early treatment is carried out. Burgundy mixture is a much more phytotoxic material formulated from copper and washing soda and is usually used as a last resort on potato blight or vine diseases.

Lime sulphur similarly is phytotoxic and is perhaps better used as a winter wash to reduce the level of fungal problems by attacking the fungi when the host plants are likely to be dormant. It is however sometimes used up to green bud stage on top fruit.

Sulphur is a very useful fungicide, particularly when used regularly to control mildew by its preventative activity. Similar to lime sulphur, care should be exercised when dealing with plants that are known to be sensitive to the material.

Materials used to control fungal problems are most effective when used as a preventative treatment, rather than as a curative – ie applying the chemical before the disease is in evidence. Early treatment combined with careful and clean pruning and treatment of damaged plants with a wound-sealing compound will also help to minimise fungal problems, along with clearing up plant debris. This can involve burning any damaged material that is known to be infected, rather than composting it, which can help retain the level of disease spores for the following season.

Some fungal diseases may also be minimised in effect by not growing plants too soft, using too much nitrogenous material as excessively lush foliage is more likely to be susceptible to disease. Organic cultural techniques reduce such soft growth, so the plants are therefore less susceptible to pests and diseases.

Biological control may also be used, by using a beneficial fungus (*Trichoderma viride*) which helps prevent some fungal diseases including silver leaf disease and problems arising from damage sustained by a tree or shrub, provided it is applied at the earliest opportunity.

Mealy bugs

Mealy bugs are a most curious pest that are more likely to be a pest problem of houseplants and plants grown under protected cultivation, especially in conservatories, than on garden plants.

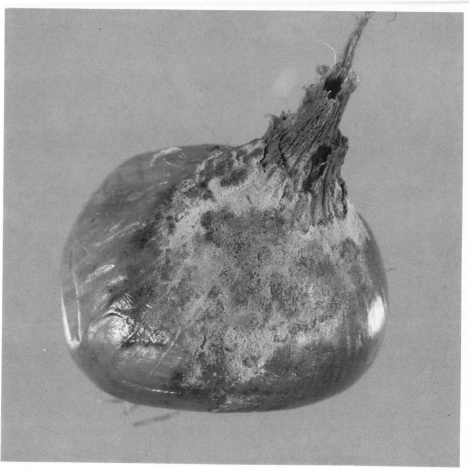

However, during warm summers mealy bugs can be a problem particularly of plants that may be grown outside during the summer such as begonia, pelargoniums, bay trees and jasmine.

The pest is most often seen as two forms, the mealy bug which infests upper parts of the plant and the root mealy bug which infests the root zone of plants, especially of those grown in pots or containers. They are odd-looking insects that as adults resemble a tiny armadillo-like creature covered with a white waxy covering which helps to protect the insect. White woolly

Above:
Neck rot of an onion caused by botrytis or grey mould fungus. This fungus can live on dead or living plant tissue and can be very dangerous to plants.
Crown Copyright

patches are often seen on the undersides of leaves or in leaf axils. Although adults may be found in the wool, most often the young are normally found hidden there in batches of around 100.

The young then feed like the adults by jabbing their pointed stylets into the soft plant tissue to absorb sap. Initially the damage caused is relatively minor, but as the population increases the damage becomes increasingly severe with deformation of leaves and even blinding-out of young shoots and flower buds.

In the case of root mealy bug infestations, the damage is less easily identified as being caused by the pest. Initially plants take on a starved, yellowing appearance and increasingly lose vigour and suffer severe checking of growth. If the plant is pot grown, careful removal will show the pest around the root ball with white powder staining of the inside of the pot and masses of white wool and feeding adults amongst the roots. Many house plants are infested by the pest including aphelandra, dracaena, cissus, rhoicissus, croton, poinsettia, ficus, cacti and other succulents, philodendron, bougainvillaea, orchids, kentia, and other palms.

Adult male mealy bugs fly, but are not always necessary as the females are quite capable of reproducing on their own throughout the year. Temperature has a direct effect upon the length of the life cycle, which obviously tends to be shorter in the summer than in the winter.

● **Control:** Mealy bugs are not easy to control and generally need several treatments to get on top of the situation. Minor infestations may be physically removed or spot treated with a cottonwool swab soaked in methylated spirits which is dabbed generously onto the masses of white wool and any adults that are seen.

Alternatively, the pest may be controlled with repeated applications of soft soap (Savona). It may be necessary to treat every 10 to 14 days to gain control.

Root mealy bugs are perhaps more difficult to control as they cannot be seen. Dipping in a soft soap solution every two to four weeks may help control the pest, but extra care should be taken to avoid causing any damage to the infested plant.

Where infestations have been severe, mealy bugs exude quite large amounts of honeydew which in turn attracts sooty mould which will need to be removed to reduce the defacing effect of the mould. Severely damaged shoots or stems may be best removed and burnt as these can be particularly difficult to effectively clean up and encourage to re-grow.

Mice

Mice can be a real nuisance pest causing particular damage to bulbs, seeds and plant material stored over the winter in sheds or outbuildings. They can also be a domestic nuisance and eat anything from carpets to electric wiring as well as foodstuffs.

As mice may take newly planted seeds as large as pea seeds, the loss of them may sometimes be blamed on pigeons, except they tend to cause less disturbance. They seem to cause most damage from autumn to early spring, when natural food reserves are low and the rodent seeks hidden food stores in the form of seed, bulbs, harvested crops and winter protected plants.

The rate of reproduction of mice is high with about four to 10 litters of five to six young per year, each of which become sexually mature themselves after about only two months. Although they may live for about 18 months, their reproductive potential is enormous.

● **Control:** Probably the easiest way to reduce the problem of mice is to keep a cat, as even the smell of a cat tends to deter mice. Alternatively, the leaves of the common spearmint (*Mentha spicata*) help to deter mice when placed close to sensitve areas. Chamomile (*Matricaria chamomilla*) may also be used as well as spurge (*Euphorbia lactea* and *E . lathyrus*) to help act as a deterrent.

Trapping is also an effective means of control and the self-setting metal traps seem to be particularly sensitive and

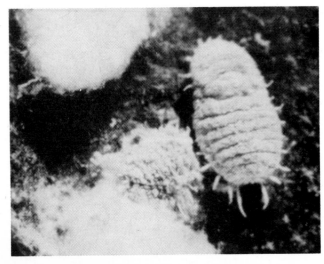

Right:
Mealy bugs are curious pests that are often seen as white powdery woodlouse-like creatures with the young incubated in white woolly patches.

highly responsive. Baiting with chocolate appears to be a useful method of attracting them and the chocolate can easily be moulded on to the bait holder.

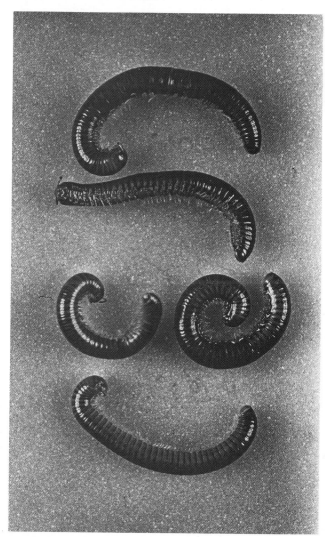

For those not wishing to actually dispatch the mice, traps are available which capture them alive, allowing them to be removed to a situation well away from the home and garden. The Longworth trap is widely used by naturalists to study small animals and if used properly captures mice without causing them any harm.

Millipedes

Take care not to confuse the more active centipede, which is a beneficial insect with the millipede which is a pest. Millipedes are much slower moving and although they tend to live on decaying organic matter and dead plants, they can equally become a pest, especially by attacking seedlings and other plants below soil level. This results in stunting, yellowing and sometimes premature death of the attacked plant or plants.

● **Control:** As the pest is active below soil level, it is difficult to control with organic, contact pesticides. It is therefore better to keep the level of plant debris to the minimum, to reduce the amount of cover and food for the pest. Regular digging will also help to expose the pest which can then be dispatched or banished to the compost heap.

Left:
Round millipedes are only usually seen when a problem has occurred and the pest is causing a great deal of damage. *Crown Copyright*

Below:
Flat millipedes are another damaging pest that can be difficult to control.
Crown Copyright

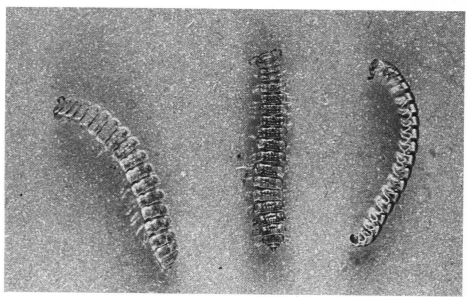

Right:
Millipede attacking a potato tuber causing the vegetable to be completely inedible and useless. *Crown Copyright*

Below right:
Red spider or two-spotted spider mites are tiny mites that are best observed with a magnifying lens.

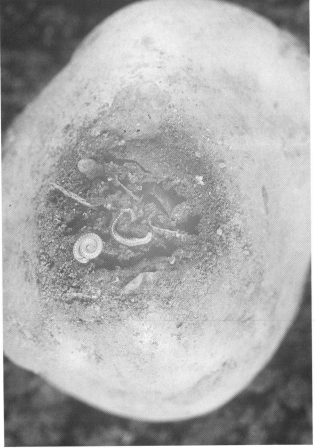

Most often the pest remains unobserved until the damage becomes apparent, which by then signifies that the population of the pest has already become quite high.

Most mites feed on the undersides of leaves although bryobia mites tend to feed on the upper leaf surfaces. As the population increases, mites can be seen more clearly and in the case of red spider mite can be observed moving back and forth along the fine webbing that they produce.

The most commonly known mite is the red spider mite or two-spotted spider mite, which is a pest of plants grown inside and out, although it is particularly damaging in the dry air conditions found indoors or under glass. The pest attacks a wide range of plants from hedera (ivy), impatiens, croton, ficus, fuchsia and cacti to cucumbers and tomatoes. The pest is actually straw or buff coloured and is only red just prior to hibernating in any areas of cover that it can find. Plants grown indoors may suffer all around the year as the pest may not hibernate, but continues to parasitise the plant because its life cycle is extended due to warmer temperatures.

Fruit tree red spider mites are a real nuisance on top and soft fruit, as the pest successfully over-winters its eggs on infested plants resulting in a rapid re-infestation the following spring.

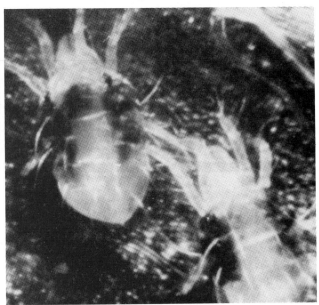

Mites

There are many types of mites which live on plants, both as parasites of plants as well as other species which are predators of other mites and insects. Both beneficial and parasitic mites are small creatures with four pairs of legs rather than insects which have three pairs of legs and this is a useful method of identifying them.

Plant parasitic mites are very tiny and extremely difficult to see with the naked eye and are best observed with a hand lens.

Bryobia mites feed on various ornamental and fruit plants and some not only over-winter as adults or eggs, but also reproduce without the need of males. The pest also feeds on upper and lower leaf surfaces.

The damage caused by most mites is very similar in that discoloration and a general lack of lustre is shown by the plant. This is followed by distinct yellowing and browning of the leaves giving a marbling effect. Premature leaf drop is quite common as infestations become severe and where web-forming mites are evident, such as red spider mite, the webbing becomes clearly visible and a mass of fine web covers the plant, particularly the growing shoots.

Dwarf conifers such as *Picea glauca* 'Albertiana Conica' exhibit a dramatic reaction to the pest by rapidly shedding their needles, rendering the plant grossly disfigured. This damage may never be recovered from by the plant, even after several years and the infested plant may have to be dug up and disposed of.

The minute tarsonemid mite is even harder to see and tends to be more active on young growth and buds. The infested plant takes on a hardened, stunted appearance with severe deformation ruining the appearance of such plants as African violets, ficus, cyclamen and strawberries.

During the winter the life cycle becomes longer, but the pest continues to be a problem, especially indoors where its presence can go unnoticed until the damage is seen. Sadly, because the pest attacks the delicate young tissue, the level of damage is likely to be high even when the population is relatively low.

Gall mites are very tiny, similar to the tarsonemid mite and these produce swellings or galls. Damage is not normally too severe except on blackcurrants where 'big-bud' is a problem caused by the mites feeding within the buds.

● **Control:** Mites are usually extremely difficult to control, especially as they tend to feed in places where it is difficult to spray effectively.

Spraying with derris may help to control adults, providing spraying is carried out thoroughly and regularly at 10 to 14-day intervals or so. Where possible spraying with lime sulphur as a winter wash may help to keep populations down by killing over-wintering mites.

Alternatively, cultural techniques in pruning-out and burning badly infested branches, washing or spraying foliage with water (mites hate water) or biological control may be used using the red spider mite predator (*Phytoseiulus persimilis*) under glass.

Left:
Big bud is caused by a tiny member of the mite family.

Moles

It does seem a shame that moles appear to always be considered as pests, particularly as they do eat quite a large number of pests themselves including slugs, caterpillars and larvae. Moles can however be a problem, not only of lawns where their molehills are unsightly and their runs likely to subside, but also of newly planted beds where young plants can be undermined or ejected. This results in the young plants dying as a result of the disturbance, or at the very least being severely checked.

Moles are likely to be more of a problem on light soils where they can tunnel freely.

● **Control:** Although moles can be effectively controlled with mole traps placed in the runs, serious consideration should be given to deterring them rather than killing them.

Camphor placed in the runs may help to chase them off and may even deter them from entering the garden in the first place if small pieces are buried every 30cm (1ft) or so at a depth of 5-7.5cm (2-3in) – which may be considered impractical.

As another form of deterrent the spurge (*Euphorbia lactea*) may also help to dissuade the mole when planted around the garden at a spacing of every 5-6m (16-20ft) or so. Moles are very susceptible to strong smells such as garlic, rags soaked in paraffin and even old fish heads are said to have some effect.

Rabbits

Rabbits can be a real problem particularly if the garden is exposed to open space. They can cause serious damage to very many plants from the smallest newly planted vegetable to shrubs and young trees.

Rabbits can strip the bark from some trees which can ring-bark the affected plant resulting in its death.

● **Control:** As wild rabbits normally enter domestic gardens on foraging excursions, one has little control over their breeding activities and population control. The main and really only effective method of preventing damage to garden plants is therefore to exclude rabbits from the garden using a wire fence, part of which should be buried to help prevent entry by burrowing. This may mean a fence of about 75cm (2ft 6in) above the ground and 45cm (1ft 6in) below ground to offer some protection.

Guard plants of foxglove (*Digitalis purpurea*) are said to help, but these have limited effect and fencing is really the only effective answer. Also to some extent a dog can dissuade rabbits from the garden.

Newly planted trees that would be otherwise exposed should also be protected by tree-guards or wire netting wrapped loosely around supported by a stake or stakes.

Scale insects

Scale insects are most unusual creatures which parasitise plants and often go unnoticed because of their unusual appearance. The insect feeds on stems and leaves of plants and looks very much like part of the plant as small raised blisters that are most often straw-coloured or brown in appearance.

Some forms of scale insects reproduce without the need of males and have a further unusual characteristic in that the eggs are protected under the mother's scale until they hatch. After the mother dies they move out like a small army of ranks of tiny pale-coloured nymphs. These progress to their feeding site which, once selected, they settle down onto like a limpit and insert their sharp stylet to suck plant sap.

Damage is usually manifested by loss of vigour, yellowing and deformation of growth as the population becomes increasingly severe. Honeydew is produced followed by sooty mould, which then becomes an unsightly nuisance. The spread of infestations is quite often by contact with other plants or from propagation of infested plant material.

A wide range of plants can be affected from cultivated garden plants such as euonymus, laurel, and many other shrubs and trees to a wide range of houseplants including palms, aphelandra, croton, dracaena, ficus and orchids.

● **Control:** Scale insects are difficult to control because of the protection afforded by the waxy scale covering for the individual insects and their eggs.

Spraying with derris or soft soap (Savona) may help to control some of the insects, especially the juveniles. However, where attacks are small and localised, physically scraping off the scales is very effective, though check again every so often for further insects.

On larger plants and where the infestation is more extensive, spraying will need to be carried out more regularly at about 10 to 14-day intervals until the various stages of the insects' life cycle have been treated.

Alternatively, biological control may have to be relied upon with the various wasps, flies, bugs or birds such as blue tits.

Slugs and snails

Slugs and snails can be a real menace in the garden, particularly during a wet season or in shady or damp parts of the garden. Their appetite is enormous and they strip leaves and stems with their curious rough tongue called a radula. Not only do they consume living plant tissue, but also dead and decaying organic matter.

However, it is their effects on lettuce, brassicas, hostas, delphinium and many other plants that they are mostly disliked for, as they can completely obliterate a plant or even a crop in a very short space of time. Feeding at night, their activity is betrayed the following morning to the abject horror of the gardener.

Slugs and snails are hermaphrodite and yet although they have male and female characteristics still cross-fertilise each other. Slugs and snails hide under litter in the garden, especially where it is moist under flagstones, pots, seed-trays, plastic bags and fallen leaves.

● **Control:** Trying to reduce the amount of cover for slugs and snails may be found to be effective in helping to keep numbers down, by clearing up leaf litter and removing pots, seed-trays etc.

Trapping them by using large leaves placed near damaged plants may encourage them to hide underneath to be exposed and disposed of the following morning, possibly on the compost heap.

A beer trap is also effective by using a jam jar, glass dish or saucer with beer in the receptacle which should be placed level with the surrounding soil. Attracted by the beer the slugs and snails start to drink and then fall in and drown. Also physically remove them as you come across them in the garden. Look for their slime trails and find them hiding on the shady side of walls and under the leaves of plants.

Guard plants such as sage (*Salvia officinalis*), hyssop, or thyme may help, as may placing coarse grit around endangered plants, but do not underestimate the biological control offered by hedgehogs, frogs and toads.

Alternatively, aluminium sulphate may be used to kill them by desiccating them, drying up the organs that produce slime.

Suckers

Suckers, especially apple and pear suckers, are particularly problematic as nymphs when the young feed on the leaves and buds early in the spring. The flying adults and nymphs suck the sap from plants causing deformed growth and sometimes premature leaf or blossom drop.

Left:
Scale insects are extraordinary pests that look like small blisters on the plant stem or leaves.

Below:
Slugs and snails are greedy nocturnal feeders that cause massive damage to leaves, stems and even bulbs and tubers. *Crown Copyright*

Honeydew is usually evident followed by sooty mould which further disfigures the infected plant. At the end of the season eggs are laid to over-winter the pest until the following year.

● **Control:** Spraying with pyrethrum or derris will control the pest. Otherwise one may have to rely on the anthocorid bug, which would be hard pressed to control a sizeable infestation.

Thrips

Perhaps more commonly known as thunder flies, thrips damage flower buds particularly, as well as leaves with both the larvae and adults causing the damage.

The small slender insects also predate on plant pests such as aphids and mites, but it is thrips such as carnation thrips, pea thrips and onion thrips that cause damage to plants. The damage takes the form of tiny marks and streaks on the infested parts, with sometimes a silvery appearance. Severe attacks cause deformation and discoloration of foliage, as well as premature leaf and flower drop.

Over-wintering occurs by various stages of the pest finding shelter amongst leaf litter or in the garden soil.

● **Control:** Pyrethrum is particularly active against thrips, but derris may also be used.

Virus diseases

Virus diseases can cause a very wide range of symptoms from deformation of the leaf, variegation, stunting, mosaic patterning, and yellowing and general wasting of the plant. Yield and growth pattern can be seriously disturbed and the results can only get worse and spread. Premature leaf-drop, wilting and even cankers can also occur.

Below:
Adult pear sucker feed like the larva by sucking plant sap.
Crown Copyright

Right:
A virus disease affecting celery, causing spotting of the foliage. Virus diseases are probably more common than we realise, but cannot be controlled other than by destruction of infected plants. *Crown Copyright*

Although some viruses can be tolerated, in that some of the effects are considered by gardeners to be attractive, others are serious problems. Amongst these are blackcurrant reversion virus which reduces the fruit yield, lettuce big vein which slightly affects yield, lily virus which stunts the growth and spoils the plant, potato virus X and potato virus Y both affecting yield and many others.

● **Control:** Sadly the control of virus diseases on infected plants is not possible. The best form of action is therefore to prevent the spread of the disease. Apart from attempting to cultivate and propagate virus-free plants and those that may be virus resistant, it is also imperative to control vectors of the virus. These are organisms that can spread the disease in the same way that the mosquito spreads malaria.

Aphids are especially dangerous as vectors and if virus prevention becomes an important criterion in crop care, a regular preventative spraying programme should be introduced, using such materials as pyrethrum or derris.

Weevils

Looking something like a beetle with a long snout-like protruberance and indistinguishable larvae, these members of the beetle family are very numerous. Adult and larval stages of weevils can be a nuisance to plants such as apples, which have their blossom attacked by the larvae of the apple blossom weevil.

Other species can be far more serious in the amount of damage caused. Vine weevil larvae for example feed upon the roots of many plants including cyclamen, gloxinia and many house plants and container-grown plants even including conifers.

Pea and bean weevil adults feed on the leaves causing small holes to appear. Some weevils hibernate on the plant as is the case on apples, or many alternatively pupate and hibernate in the soil.

● **Control:** Treating with derris either as a spray or dust may help to control weevils attacking foliage.

Weevils that are active at soil level or below soil level are far more difficult to control and rogueing out infested plants to be dipped in a solution of pyrethrum, or alternatively destroying them, may be found to be the only really effective means of control.

Whitefly

Whitefly are small white moth-like insects that can be a pest indoors and outside. On their favourite plants such as cucumber, tomato, poinsettia, fuchsia and pelargonium they can be a real nuisance indoors or under glass. Outside brassicas in particular may be attacked and infested.

The damage resulting is relatively minor for the nuisance factor of the insects, but some discoloration may occur as well as the disfiguration caused by sooty mould growing on the honeydew excreted by the feeding nymphs.

Eggs are laid on the leaf undersides and develop into feeding nymphs which grow to look like greyish-white scale-like objects. These scales are covered with a waxy cuticle which helps protect the insect from sprays. The insect can over-winter as adults or pupae, although the pest continues to breed on plants grown indoors.

● **Control:** Due to the somewhat extended life cycle of the pest, it is essential to spray regularly with pyrethrum, derris or soft soap (Savona) to kill as many adults as possible prior to

Above:
Pea and bean weevils cause holes to appear in leaves which are very evident and easily identify the culprit.
Crown Copyright

Right:
Whitefly adult and feeding scales on leaf underside. A large population can be a nuisance and can reduce vigour.
Crown Copyright

them laying more eggs. The nymphs are difficult to kill with insecticides and after pupation emerge as adults.

Biological control using *Encarsia formosa* wasps may be worth considering for use under glass, where the parasite may help to keep the pest at a more tolerable level.

Wireworm

The relatively long-lived larvae of the click-beetle can live for four to five years in the soil where this slender buff-coloured larvae attacks potato tubers, strawberries, brassicas and many other vegetable plants, as well as cultivated plants including chrysanthemums, dahlias and gladioli.

After the larval stage the insect pupates and emerges as an adult to lay eggs in the early summer.

● **Control:** Wireworms are extremely difficult to control with organic insecticides and are perhaps best controlled by cultural techniques including regular digging and cultivation to expose the pest.

Woodlice

Woodlice are actually land-living crustaceans that need to live in moist dank conditions, feeling particularly at home amongst dead and decaying organic matter, especially rotting wood. The light to mid-grey-coloured creatures prefer dark conditions and shelter from the light, preferring to feed at night.

Although mostly a scavenging creature, they can nevertheless become a pest, particularly of young plants and seedlings. A favourite way to attract them to cause damage is to grow seedlings in old wooden seed-trays left on the ground out of direct light. The resultant seedlings are not only likely to etiolate and weaken, but also to be readily attacked by woodlice which attack roots, stems and leaves.

Eggs are usually laid amongst decaying organic matter and plant debris and rubbish, on hatching the young wood louse is then ready to join the colony in its activity.

● **Control:** The best method to control woodlice is to be a tidier gardener, taking care to clear up plant debris and to ensure seed-trays are clean and sound before use.

Where colonies are localised away from plants, they can be speedily dispatched with boiling water if so wished. If the colony is evenly spread, it can be localised by laying down a piece of soft rotting wood, or a plastic sack with some decomposing leaf litter underneath. The colony can then be removed or destroyed.

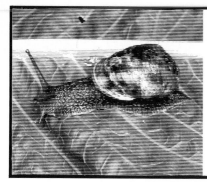

7 Health and Safety

Although organic pesticides are often considered to be 'safe' products, care should always be taken over their handling, use, storage and disposal. Even though organic materials are considered to be better for the environment, they are nevertheless poisonous chemicals and should be treated with absolute respect. Just because the chemical is of organic origin does not mean that it can be abused or can be used without taking account of any hazards associated with it.

Whilst not wishing to terrify the potential user of organic pesticides, they should nevertheless be regarded in the same way as any other chemical of a similar toxic level. It is perhaps a somewhat sobering thought to consider that many of the most toxic chemicals and substances are of natural origin. Ricin obtained from the seed of the castor oil plant (*Ricinus communis*) is extremely toxic and is believed to be the chemical that was used a few years ago to assassinate a foreign agent, a minute drop being injected by means of a sword-stick and which proved to be fatal. Many other plants including fungi are known to be poisonous, varying in the level of toxicity from mild to fatal, with some having long-term effects from prolonged exposure resulting in carcinogenic hazards.

It is therefore imperative to treat any chemical, whether organic or not with the greatest respect and care and to follow the chemical manufacturer's instructions as well as the code of practice from the Ministry of Agriculture, Fisheries and Food.

Firstly, it may seem obvious, but before doing anything, read the chemical label thoroughly. Surprisingly, many people do not bother and therefore fail to follow the recommendations made. Take particular account of what protective equipment and clothing is needed and what safety precautions should be observed. Timing of spraying, dilution ratio or other forms of application is important to minimise environmental damage

and to effect the best possible measure of control. Taking account of the frequency of spraying necessary to gain control is also important, and you may need to keep records of when next to treat the infested crop.

Having read the label thoroughly and taken account of all of the implications, ensure that the correct protective clothing is worn before even removing the cap from the can or bottle. The absolute minimum should be a pair of industrial gloves, as chemical concentrates can be extremely poisonous. Nicotine for example is deadly and can be readily absorbed into the body through the skin. Therefore be sure that the gloves are of the right specification and are water- and chemical-proof as well as being free from any holes or tears.

It is a sensible idea to wear a face mask over the mouth and nose to prevent inhalation or ingestion and protective goggles to prevent splashes into the eyes. Their use is worthwhile, even for the safest chemical to be safe rather than sorry.

The chemical should then be mixed as recommended, taking particular care to use exactly the right amount. Using too little can result in a poor effect and with certain chemicals the risk of resistance building up. Using too much is not only wasteful, but can be phytotoxic, or in other words, it can seriously damage the plants onto which it is sprayed. Some chemicals can cause damage to certain plants when applied as recommended by the chemical manufacturer, due to sensitivity of the plant. This point must be checked before treatment.

The material should therefore be used exactly as directed. It is wise not to experiment with novel techniques that could result in a risk to the user, or to the plants being treated.

Exercise particular care to ensure that spray drift is minimised and of course if possible avoided altogether. Try to spray only during calm weather and not when it is windy. If it is even

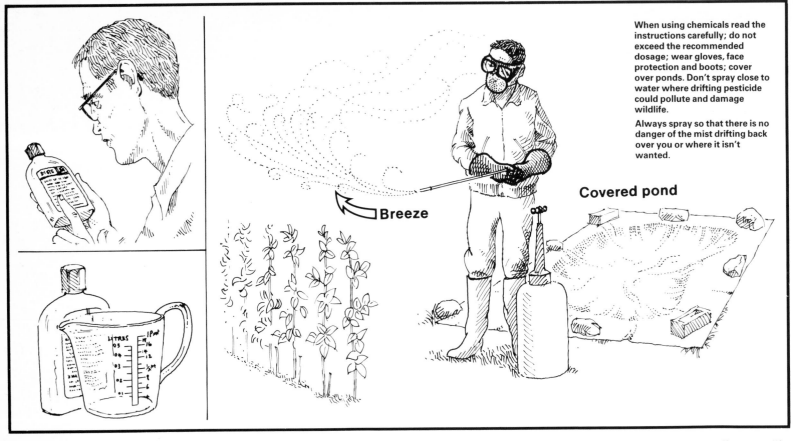

When using chemicals read the instructions carefully; do not exceed the recommended dosage; wear gloves, face protection and boots; cover over ponds. Don't spray close to water where drifting pesticide could pollute and damage wildlife.

Always spray so that there is no danger of the mist drifting back over you or where it isn't wanted.

Breeze

Covered pond

slightly breezy, take care to avoid spraying where the wind can blow the drift back over yourself or where it could have damaging effects, such as drifting over a pond or stream.

It is essential to ensure that chemicals are only applied where you want them and are not allowed to spread all over the place where their effect upon the local environment could be damaging. Remember that even organic chemicals can kill beneficial insects and careless use can seriously disturb the natural balance.

Spray drift can be particularly damaging to watercourses, streams, rivers and ponds. The tiniest amount of insecticide being blown onto a pond can have a devastating effect upon life, starting with the pond life and in particular fish which quickly die in the event. Where this happens comes the added danger of the poison getting into food chains, thereby causing damage beyond the limits of the pond.

A further point to remember is that poisons usually take much longer to break down to safer products in water than when they are deposited onto plant foliage. If plants have to be treated and there is even the smallest risk of spray drift, it is worthwhile covering the pond with a sheet of polythene or a tarpaulin. However, having done this, immediately rinse off the sheet with clean water as any residue laying on the sheet could pollute the pond the next time the sheet is used and is mistakenly inverted and the chemical residue released.

When measuring concentrated chemicals, take care not to spill the material. If this does occur, wash the spillage away with copious amounts of water to reduce the potential hazard. It is also prudent to rinse the container or bottle as tiny dribbles of chemical running down the side of the container could be hazardous, especially if the container is picked up and handled with an ungloved hand.

A particularly dangerous practice, which should never be carried out is the transfer of a chemical to another container for

When you've finished with chemicals, wipe the containers clean and clear up spillages rinsing well with water.

Always store chemicals out of reach of children and in their original containers. *Never* decant them into other containers.

Poisonous chemicals should be stored securely under lock and key.

Powders and dusts may be kept in a polythene bag to help prevent damage from damp.

storage. Many people, including children, have been poisoned and in some cases have died by accidentally ingesting chemicals that have been incorrectly stored in such containers as cola bottles, sherry bottles or beer bottles. This practice has been particularly known to be a problem when large economy size containers have been purchased and their contents shared amongst friends. Chemicals must be stored in their original container bearing the correct identification of the product together with its instructions for use.

Once used, the chemical container should be adequately and securely sealed before being safely stored. Ensure that the material is stored where it is as safe as possible and out of harm's reach. It should be kept well away from foodstuffs and away from where children, pets, wildlife or any unauthorised person could gain access to it.

A garden shed may seem ideal, but is it always kept locked? Also are the shelves high enough? Maybe the garage is a safer place where it can be stored under lock and key on a high shelf with other chemicals, paints, wood preservatives and car polish etc.

Quite a few chemicals are photosensitive, or in other words are broken down by sunlight. Pyrethroids are examples of this and even when stored in dark glass bottles, they should be kept away from light, which may mean that account needs to be taken of daylight entering the storage area through a window. For this reason, as well as the fact that a glasshouse is unlikely to be kept securely locked, one should not store chemicals in such a place.

Not all chemicals are liquids and where formulations are in crystalline or powder form, consideration will need to be given to the effect of moisture, as damp conditions can deteriorate a chemical's effectiveness. To reduce the chance of this happening, it may be worth placing such chemicals inside a polythene bag or airtight container, whilst keeping the chemical within its own packaging.

When handling or applying chemicals, it is essential to use appropriate protective clothing such as a face mask, face shield or goggles and industrial rubber or neoprene gloves. Protective equipment such as this should really be used for even the most apparently inoffensive chemicals to help prevent any possible accident.

When chemicals such as nicotine are handled, it is important to ensure that even greater care is exercised and that an improved level of protective clothing is used. A waterproof jacket or coat made from PVC and even a sou'wester hat can be useful when spraying such chemicals, especially on trees and bushes where spray mist or droplets could easily contaminate the person spraying. It may even be sensible to use PVC trousers and Wellington boots, with the protective trousers worn over the boots to prevent chemical droplets running down into the boots.

Although all of this may seem somewhat excessive, it is far better to wear more protective clothing and equipment than too little. It is also essential to ensure that the equipment is well maintained and kept scrupulously clean on the inside as well as the outside. Not only should face-mask filters be regularly changed, but all protective clothing should be thoroughly washed after being used and safely stored where it cannot be damaged or torn.

Even if the correct protective clothing has been worn, it is essential that hands and any exposed skin are well washed after any chemical use. Although materials such as pyrethrum are fairly safe to handle, much greater care needs to be taken with such chemicals as nicotine, particularly because of its very high level of dermal toxicity (ability to poison directly through the skin). For this reason it is essential to avoid all possible contact with the chemical. Even the slightest exposure of the skin to dilute chemical or smoke can result in reddening and acute sensitising of the skin at the very least. Obviously, in such a situation any accidental contact with the chemical should be followed immediately by washing thoroughly with soap and water. However, due to the toxicity of nicotine it is advisable not to use it and to use a safer alternative.

When spraying or chemical application has been completed, it may be found necessary to dispose of surplus chemical. When this happens, it is essential not to simply pour the chemical into a drain or away in some other thoughtless manner. Unfortunately, once chemicals have been mixed into solution, they can rarely be stored for more than a few hours due to the likelihood of deterioration. Besides, it is unwise to leave chemicals around even in dilute form.

In disposing of the surplus chemical, carefully select a site in the form of an area of waste land or garden. This should be well away from watercourses, streams, ponds or where children, pets or wildlife could be accidentally exposed and endangered. Even pouring chemicals on to a site well away from areas that are deemed sensitive will result in some localised damage to the environment and will kill beneficial organisms. All one can do is to minimise the level of damage by a little thought. Simply pouring the chemical down the drain is also not the solution, as the poison will still end up somewhere that it is not intended.

Having disposed of the surplus chemical solution, the sprayer should be thoroughly washed out and the rinsings disposed of in the same careful manner as previously mentioned.

Even chemical containers need to be disposed of carefully and should be thoroughly washed out before being thrown away.

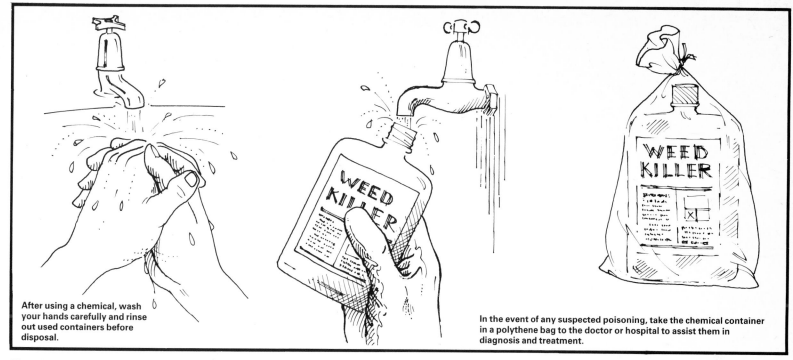

After using a chemical, wash your hands carefully and rinse out used containers before disposal.

In the event of any suspected poisoning, take the chemical container in a polythene bag to the doctor or hospital to assist them in diagnosis and treatment.

Tins should be perforated or crushed to prevent them being used for other purposes and together with glass bottles placed in the refuse bin. On no account should aerosol containers be punctured or incinerated, as this is extremely dangerous and severe injury could result from an explosion.

Chemical containers should never ever be used for purposes other than for which they were intended and must be safely disposed of after use.

Where chemicals have been used, keep children, people and pets away from the area; and do not enter or consume any plants until after the safety interval recommended, even if thoroughly washed as plants must be anyway.

Finally, if ever the most unfortunate incident should occur, that somebody accidentally ingests or is otherwise exposed to a chemical with the possible result of poisoning, it is imperative to act immediately. The local hospital casualty department should be contacted and any person affected by the chemical conveyed to the casualty department immediately. It is also essential to take the chemical container in a polythene bag to enable accurate identification and treatment to be arranged. Chemical names can be easily confused and although most organic chemicals are generally considered safer than man-made materials, products such as nicotine are extremely toxic and correct treatment to exposure is imperative without delay.

The Future

Environmental issues are likely to increase in importance and organic methods of crop production will certainly become more popular. As knowledge grows it is also likely that many new biological control organisms and methods will be introduced. Legislation will also change and some of the current products may be discontinued. To this end take full account of the most current information and especially the Food and Environment Protection Act (1987) and any revisions, as well as advice from the Ministry of Agriculture, Fisheries and Food.

Useful Addresses

Chase Organics Ltd,
Coombelands House, Coombelands Lane, Addlestone,
Weybridge KT15 1HY

Suppliers of: Vegetable and flower seeds, organic fertilisers and pesticides, 'Agryl' P17 fleece and a good range of green manure seeds

Elm Farm Research Centre,
Hamstead Marshall, Berkshire RG15 0HR

Soil analysis service

Henry Doubleday Research Association,
National Centre for Organic Gardening, Ryton-on-Dunsmore,
Coventry CV8 3LG

Members of the HDRA receive a free quarterly newsletter and free entrance to Ryton Gardens. The HDRA is Britain's largest organic gardening organisation

Suppliers of: Wide range of seeds, organic fertilisers, pesticides and sundries

The Soil Association Ltd,
86-88 Colston Street, Bristol, Avon BS1 5BB

The Soil Association's Symbol scheme acts as a consumer guarantee of quality. Members receive a free quarterly magazine which covers subjects such as organic farming, food quality and dangers of pesticides

Further Reading

C. Algar; *The Chase Organics Gardening Manual*, Ian Allan Ltd, 1989.

C. Algar; *The Chase Organics Book of Fruit and Vegetable Cultivation*, Ian Allan Ltd, 1989.

A. Algar; *The Organic Allotment*; Ian Allan Ltd, 1990.

Laurence D. Hills; *Pest Control Without Poisons*; Henry Doubleday Research Association.

Cassells Encyclopaedia.

Pesticide Handbook; British Crop Protection Council.

Greet Buchner & Fieke Hoogvelt; *Nature On Your Side*; Pan.

Agricultural Development and Advisory Service Leaflets; Ministry of Agriculture, Fisheries and Food.

Jim Hay; *Natural Pest And Disease Control*; Century.

Stefan Buczacki & Keith Harris; *Collins Guide To The Pests, Diseases And Disorders Of Garden Plants*; Collins.

Field Guide To The Animals Of Britain; Readers Digest.

Michael Chinery; *Field Guide To The Insects Of Britain And Northern Europe*; Collins.

Index